Throwing Back the Chair

NINO FROSTINO

DEDICATION

To my wife Donna, the heart and soul of my life for her
unconditional love, support, and encouragement through
my entire career

To my daughters Michelle and Jennifer, for their profound love
of their mother and support throughout the years

To my son Michael, for the cherished love and respect we have for
each other

To my Mom and Dad, Helen and Phil Bova, who were great role
models. I hope you are proud of me

To my brother Frank, my best friend, advisor, traveling
companion and loyal supporter

To my sister Phyllis, for always supporting me. I will never forget
the single engine flight to Notre Dame

To the "Divine Nine" Nicholas, Christopher, Olivia, Luke, Brooke,
Lauren, Michael, Jake and Kayley, I am a truly blessed
grandfather

CONTENTS

ACKNOWLEDGMENTS

To Nino Frostino, my author for his total commitment, loyalty, and dedication to completing this book

To Dan Largent, dear friend, coach, author and strong advisor, while completing his own book

To Nancy Gulden, for your friendship and editing prowess

To Bob Garn, one of my protégés and good friends, for driving to games while I slept and re-energized

To John Furchill, for being a man of his word

To Michael Reghi, for his unending support and encouragement

To Jim Delvecchio, Bobby Brown, Respected Officials in Cleveland that prepared me for college basketball

To London Bradley and Fred Jaspers, for a job well done

To my West High School Teammates and dear friends that I have cherished over the years

To Al Drews, Dave Kuhn, and Mike Holzheimer for their encouragement to write this memoir

To my Buckeye High School Colleagues, Friends and Former Students that have supported me for 35 years

To my St. Edward High School Athletes and Community, for assisting me in my development

1

FOREWORD

Following a dream, a passion, in one's life takes many a turn, with obstacles built in, on very challenging roads.

Phil Bova chronicles a dominant spirit and the will necessary to achieve, as life unfolds around him, in "Throwing Back the Chair", his climb to college basketball refereeing prominence.

Bova is a winner in every phase of life, and his methods to achieve, and major steps in the process, will serve as inspiration to all who seek bigger and better accomplishment in their lives.

Filled with personal stories, in game and off court, involving many of the biggest names, coaches and players, from the world of college basketball, Bova's insights, memories, and musings are sure to invoke many a fond college hoops memory for readers and fans alike.

All the coaching scowls, light hearted moments, heated arguments, and the friendships that ultimately endured, make "Throwing Back the Chair" slam dunk reading for all!

-Michael Reghi
Veteran ESPN College Basketball Play-by-Play Broadcaster

"We don't need refs, but I guess white guys need something to do."

-Charles Barkley

1

<u>Thanks, Cleveland Browns</u>

The home team has the ball in the waning seconds. It's been a tight game throughout the night between these two heated rivals. There are at least 15,000 in the stands as everyone waits in anticipation to see how the final moments will play out. After the timeout, the players head to the floor.

The point guard has the ball and knows they need a bucket to erase this one point deficit and win the ball game. The shot clock is turned off—there just isn't enough time on the clock to run it before the buzzer sounds. After some mild pressure and a few passes back and forth, the point guard takes the ball and deadheads to the basket in hopes of being the hero on campus that day.

After a fake to the left and a crossover dribble, he heads down the lane like a bolt of lightning. Now just a few feet away, he flips the ball toward the basket just seconds before a spectacular collision with the other team's big man, who had stepped in the lane to impede the point guard's progress. The ball clanks off the rim just as the whistle blows. All 15,000 fans, the players, coaches, ushers, ticket takers, and anything else with a pair of eyes stare at the official under the basket to see what the call is.

"CHARGE!! PLAYER CONTROL FOUL!"

5

The official has his palm on the back of his head and with a fist pointing the other direction, declares a foul on the guy that 99.5% of the people in the gym want to score.

"WE'RE GOING THE OTHER WAY!"

Needless to say, the crowd is in an uproar. Right call or not, the home team's faithful think you screwed them over, and you just ruined their weekend.

"You suck, ref!!!"

"Ref—what did they pay you to make that call?!"

"You better not hope I see you in the parking lot!"

Meanwhile, the head coach is on the verge of an aneurysm after the call. Of course, the 39 minutes and 45 seconds prior to the final play had no bearing on the outcome; YOU cost them the basketball game.

As you walk by the bench of the road team, the opposing coach yells over to you...

"Nice call, Stripes."

On the way home, the sports talk radio shows are abuzz at the outcome and the way the game ended.

"How did he get that call so wrong?"

"That official is going to cost us a spot in the tourney!"

"Clueless...that guy should be doing CYO games."

Welcome to my world.

Raise your hand if you thought to yourself as a youngster, "You know, I'd like to be a basketball referee when I grow up." That's what I thought—not too many hands up out there. Of course, doctor, astronaut, basketball PLAYER makes the list, but an official generally isn't too high on too many wish lists. Honestly, it never really crossed my mind either…but the Man Upstairs has a way of working things out for the best. And without question—that's what happened to me.

I grew up in a middle-class family in the 1950s on Cleveland's West side. Pretty normal family I would say, with a loving mother and a father who was a detective on the Cleveland Police force. Growing up, I was always a fan of all sports….football, baseball, basketball, you name it. I loved the game and loved the competitive nature. I worked hard at bettering myself as an athlete through the local CYO program at St. Coleman's and eventually took my talents (a la LeBron James) to Cleveland West High School.

The old West High School was a classic place, sitting on the corner of West 69th and Franklin and was built near the turn of the century in 1902. Back then, West was considered one of the high school powerhouse programs in the Cleveland area, always putting out solid teams until the school met its demise in 1970. The building itself was actually razed as enrollment dwindled and eventually merged with Lincoln High School. Lincoln-West High School was then established and carries on to this day.

BUT…in the 1960s is where I will take you back. As I mentioned, I was a decent athlete and was fortunate enough to not only be on the football, basketball, and baseball teams, but also be named Captain of all three squads. I wasn't THE best athlete in the school, but I believe I earned the right to lead the teams due to my 100% effort and ability to lead by example. That was important to me. Anyone can SAY they are leaders, but being named as a captain by my peers was special. In reality, it laid the foundation to some other fantastic leadership opportunities I was able to attain later in my career. We will get into that later...

I was a decent football player, nothing special, but loved to play the game. On the basketball team, I played alongside Phil Argento—probably one of the best high school players to ever come out of Cleveland. He eventually played for Adolph Rupp at Kentucky and got drafted by the Los Angeles Lakers. Needless to say, he earned the basketball spotlight at our school. A 66 point performance (before the 3-point line existed!) against Cleveland South will do that for you.

That left baseball, which was my best sport. I played shortstop for the West High Cowboy team and eventually was named All-Ohio in 1964. Great honor for an Irish/Italian kid in Cleveland... Following my time at West, I married my High School Sweetheart, Donna Cassarino, in 1966 and thought about trying to make it on the diamond. I took a job as an educator and athletic director at Our Lady of Angels Catholic School to pay the bills, and I dreamed of making it to the Bigs after a few years of putting some pennies away.

As you can probably imagine, the salary of a grade school teacher wasn't anything to write home about. I loved working with kids, but I was starting a family and needed some funds in the ol' bank account to pursue my dream. One thing led to another, and I took a couple part-time jobs working the mutual windows at the local horse tracks—Thistledown and Northfield Park. Want to plunk a few bucks down on the win/place/show or trifecta? I was your guy. I would work 10 races on Friday and Saturday night at Northfield...and do 10 on Thursday night and Saturday afternoon at Thistledown. That was good money, man...$28 per shift. I thought I was on top of the world. Mix in Sunday mass and my 9 to 5 at OLA, and it was a very busy time in my life. Working the track schedule was exhausting, but just as sure as there are steers in Texas, it sure as heck beat the job cleaning the horse stalls. I worked that grueling schedule for a couple years.

In 1968, I was invited to a charity basketball game by my friend Greg Birney. Greg was a teacher at Roehm Junior High in Berea, Ohio. That winter, the Junior High staff played some Cleveland Browns in a charity hoops game in the Roehm gym. He invited me to attend. I was a Browns fan and liked hoops, so why not? The Browns were actually good then, and it was a chance to potentially see Paul Warfield, Leroy Kelly, and Frank Ryan up close? Yep—count me in. I headed to the game intent on sitting back and having fun watching my friend take on the Brownies. Little did I know, this game would change my life completely.

The game tipped off and everything was going according to plan in the early going. Then suddenly, one of the officials turned an ankle and couldn't continue participating. The healthy official asked the crowd for a volunteer to take the place of his injured partner. You could hear crickets in that joint. I then felt this lightning bolt of inspiration go through my body. I am an athlete, I know hoops, AND I can rub elbows with my buddy Greg and the Browns? Nervously, my hand went up. I walked down to the floor, and he put the whistle around my neck.

"What's your name, son?" he asked.

"Um, it's Phil Bova, sir," I replied.

"You ever ref a game?"

"No, but I know the rules. If someone gets knocked on his

ass, I'll blow this whistle"

"Good enough, kid. When in doubt, call it against the Browns."

I had a great time. I am a take charge person. That was right up my alley, and I enjoyed the challenge of calling a game. I wasn't sure that this could be something I could make a career of, but man, did I love it. Little did I know that day would plant the seed for decades of fruit.

The following winter, February 23, 1969, Donna and I were blessed to have our first child. Michelle arrived, and so did the urgency to figure out what I was going to do with my life.

A couple months later, I finally had the opportunity to show what I could do on the baseball field. I spent some time in the Cleveland Indians farm system. I certainly had visions of grandeur, hoping to one day make it to the big club and play at Municipal Stadium. Keep in mind—this was the 60s, and ballplayer salaries were MUCH different than they are today, but still, my dream was to make a living as a professional ballplayer. The minimum salary in 1969 was $7,000 a year, while the average salary was $19,000 per season. Big money, right? Sure, a far, far cry from $4.4 million average in 2017, but times were different back then. Guys played for the love of the game and the competition, not necessarily so they could buy a small country after playing a few seasons in the league. That's what I wanted to do. Put on my Chief Wahoo cap and play for the Tribe. Now with a munchkin in the house, I really had to determine if pro ball was a legit reality.

At the same time, I remained very intrigued by the referee thing, so I decided to get my certification in 1969. I thought I could do some games when I had some free time while trying to launch my baseball career. I was lucky enough to ref some CYO games at St. Edward High School on Saturdays and Sundays, making a whopping $3 per game. I would usually do the full slate that day...doing seven straight games and putting 21 bucks in my pocket. Yep—that's correct—sitting in the Thistledown window was more lucrative than running up and down the floor arguing with coaches. I didn't care. I loved the feeling of being part of the game. I continued to take as many CYO and Junior High games as I could to earn a few bucks and gain some experience.

Well, as I mentioned a bit earlier, sometimes the plan that I had in mind didn't necessarily coincide with what You-Know-Who in the sky. I gave it my best effort for a couple years with the Tribe and after a couple seasons barely keeping my head above water, I decided to hang up my spikes and try to map out what was next in my life. I was married, had a daughter, and then Donna was due in August of 1971 with our second child. I needed to start thinking ahead. Future. Family. Finances. A challenge to be sure.

Jennifer made her entrance into our family on August 24, 1971. Along with Michelle's birth, this was one of the happiest days of my life. Now I was a father of two, and I really felt the pressure to establish myself in the professional world.

Right around the same time, I wanted to give baseball a last hurrah while playing AAA ball in Lakewood, Ohio. I was playing for the Wenham Truckers and was enjoying a great season. As you may or may not know, sandlot baseball during that era in Cleveland was of high quality and very popular. Ex-pros and college athletes made up these teams. In fact, Steve Stone, the 1980 American League Cy Young winner, pitched with Wenham at one point.

As the season was drawing to a close, our Truckers team was to take on Airmatic Valve, with the winner advancing to the National Tournament in Battle Creek, Michigan. It was a big game in the area to be sure.

That game didn't go as planned early on, but our team made a comeback toward the end to make things very interesting. Clark Gray was on the hill for Airmatic, clinging to an 8-5 lead in the 9th inning. We had Truckers on 2nd and 3rd base with 2 outs, and yours truly stepping up next.

Clark and I battled. I fought off several pitches as the tension mounted. Finally, I got the pitch I wanted and hit a line shot to the left field gap. It went all the way to the fence. I took off running like my pants were on fire.

My teammates on base scored easily as I approached 2nd base. Bud Middaugh (the head coach at Miami, Ohio at the time) was the left fielder. I looked up and saw him bobble the ball. Trying to be aggressive, I planted my foot on the bag at 2nd and kept on chugging toward 3rd. Middaugh had a rocket arm. I knew that but also knew I could make it.

I started my slide into 3rd and clearly felt I beat the ball there. I heard the umpire yell "SAFE!", but he also extended his right arm up in the air as if to make the "out" call. Jack Oring (the Airmatic 3rd Basemen) and I looked up to see what the actual call was. The umpire then decided that I was out. Needless to say, all Hell broke loose.

I was livid. Beyond reproach. As I jumped up to argue the call, I apparently bumped the umpire, which of course is a huge no-no in ANY sporting event.

Both benches cleared. My father (a Cleveland Detective)

jumped over the fence to calm me down and go after the umpire too. Tough to do at the same time! But he tried, God love him. The umpire was Joe Bunyak, ironically a guy I knew well and really liked. I just didn't like him so much on that day.

Because of the importance of this game, I am guessing Lakewood had some of its finest on hand. The reason I say that is because three police cars were on hand very quickly to break up the near riot. Remember, this is pre cell phone!

This entire fracas could have been avoided if I just stayed on 2nd where I belonged. For those baseball junkies out there, the old cliché of "don't make the 3rd out at 3rd base" couldn't have rung more true. I took us out of the game. Final score Airmatic 8, Wenham 7.

The Lakewood Baseball Commission met a couple days later and decided to ban me for life in any Lakewood League. For 44 years, I was hired to police the rules of college basketball, and in one instance in a baseball game, I broke all the rules. The crazy ending was always a teaching moment at my baseball camps.

One step further, my brother Frank's son is also named Phil Bova. That Phil Bova enjoyed a solid career playing ball at St Edward High School and at Adrian College in Michigan. He continued his love for the game playing in a men's league in—you guessed it—Lakewood. To this day, he has to prove that he is NOT me when registering for leagues. If only I had stayed at second base...

Though I was banned from Lakewood athletics, I wasn't banned from teaching and coaching. I was still teaching at OLA and was asked by Joe Mackey to coach the St Edward Freshmen team in my spare time. Of course, Coach Mackey was the legendary head coach of the Eagles at that time. Through Coach Mackey, I met Ray Dieringer and had the pleasure of picking his brain on anything basketball related. Needless to say, Ray was the hoops coach at Cleveland State at the time. Basketball was still fairly new at CSU, and Ray was trying to build the program. At the time, colleges still had JV squads that would play games before the "A" team took the floor. A year after making his acquaintance, Coach called during that 1972 season and asked if I would help out reffing a JV game before the big boys took the floor. What did I have to lose? I took him up on his offer.

I officiated that first game and worked my backside off. I gave maximum effort. Even though the attendance was about 22 people, the crowd began to grow as the varsity game drew near. The game wasn't about ME, it was still my reputation on the line. I called a solid game. I was loving what I was doing, getting a good workout in, and making $25 for my efforts. It's not rocket science, but one college JV game rewarded me more than reffing EIGHT grade school games. It was a rewarding gig if you can get it.

After that game, I headed back to the locker room to get cleaned up. As I was walking in, the officials for the Varsity game were about to head out. I was intercepted by Jim Desmond, who started officiating games in 1966. By 1968, he was on the staff of the Mid American Conference and was chosen to work this Cleveland State game.

He said, "Good game. I like the way you work"

"Phil Bova, sir, pleasure to meet you," I replied.

"Keep doing what you are doing…."

I was on Cloud Nine. I thought I was doing a good job and thought that I controlled a game pretty well. To have a 'real' official observe what I could do and comment on my work was beyond flattering. Instead of heading out with the fellas after the game for a couple beverages, I hung around for the Varsity game. I wanted to watch Desmond work. I wanted to see how he and his partner called the contest, handled coaches and managed the game. Even though this was before the shot clock era and 3-point line, there are a million things to manage in a college basketball game. Those officials were great. I watched and learned and took as many mental notes as I could. I drove home after the game and told Donna about it. When I walked in the house, I started to ramble on about the night and what I had learned She just stood there and looked at me like I had sustained a mild concussion or that I had a screw loose. When I finally paused to breathe, I waited for her to ask a million questions. She looked at me with fake excitement in her eyes and reminded me to prepare my lessons for the next week at OLA. Ugh.

A few weeks passed, and I got another call from Coach Dieringer asking if I could pinch hit in another JV game. Are you kidding me? Of course, I would.

I headed down to the old Public Hall to do the game. Again, I felt I had a really good game. Didn't think I made any mistakes, commanded the game the way it should be, and kept it moving. Hey, it was another $25. Just like the first time, I headed to the locker room to shower, and guess who passed me on the way out? Yep. Jim Desmond.

"Bova, right?"

"Yes, Sir."

This time, he just kept walking.

I took the same course of action as I did for the first CSU game. Passed on heading to the watering hole and instead watched Desmond like a hawk. The more I watched, the more I learned, and the better I would be at my job. I am a competitive guy by nature and if there was any chance I could take to better myself, I was going to take it. Observing Desmond work the game made me a better official. I went home that night as excited as I was before, kissed Donna good night, and started thinking about Our Lady of Angels. At the same time, I asked myself how I could be as good as Jim Desmond.

A few weeks later, I came home from OLA and saw a note on the counter to call John Payak. John was the Supervisor of Officials for the Mid American Conference.

John was a player at Bowling Green and was eventually inducted in the school's Hall of Fame. After spending some time in the US Navy, John played pro ball in the early 1950s in Milwaukee and Philadelphia. After retiring from the game, John became an official and eventually landed as the Supervisor of Officials for the MAC.

"Phil, the Mid-American Conference would like to bring you on board to do a handful of JV games for the 1973 season. You were highly recommended by both Jim Desmond and Ray Dieringer."

After I picked my jaw up from the floor, I knew this could be the start of something big. The Mid-American was a Division 1 conference and though it was still JV, it was a start.

"I would be honored to work for the MAC."

It didn't stop there. In the same year, I also received a call from Bobby Brown, who was the commissioner of the Ohio

Athletic Conference. He asked if I would officiate some games for the OAC as well. HELL YEAH.

Later that summer, August 23 to be exact, God blessed us with our 3rd and final child, Michael. I loved my daughters dearly, but I was glad to have a boy to add to the family. Just like most Italians, it was important to keep the Bova name moving forward to further generations. Now we are a family of five. Time to start kicking ass on the hardwood.

The 1973 season was here, and I looked forward to my OAC games and challenge in the Mid American Conference that was only five games in that first season. But I kept my skills sharp by advancing in the local ranks and doing the Division 3 OAC games. Gone were the days of marathon CYO games, and instead, I became more selective in high school games. I wanted to keep my options open in case I got the call to do more college games. While contemplating the potential of more games, I always kept my commitment to the students at Our Lady of Angels. They were the first priority. Luckily, that first season in the MAC, I had local games like Kent, Akron, and Bowling Green…so I could do games, make the drive back home, and answer the bell in the morning for class.

My scores from the supervisors of officials and coaching feedback were good that first year, and naturally, that resulted in a few more MAC games in 1974. I kept my high school games, added more Division 3 games like Baldwin Wallace and John Carroll, and kept earning side money officiating. Thank God I didn't have to work the windows at the track anymore. I had a blooming career to chase.

Fast forward another year to 1975, and I received another

call to the landline at my house. For all you young bucks, cell phones weren't around yet! It was John Payak on the line. I thought I did something wrong or my gig was up...

"Phil, we would like to offer you a position to do the Varsity games and be part of the rotation for the '75 season. Will you join us?"

I'm not sure if I pinched myself to make sure this was reality, or if I asked Donna to listen in to the conversation, but I am pretty sure I answered the same way that I did the first time.

"I would be honored to work for the MAC."

I'm going to do this.

I accepted the offer to work for the MAC, but made it clear that my commitment to teaching kids at school was the top priority. I was an educator first and foremost. I've always been proud to say that. That said, my nine year run at Our Lady of Angels came to an end, and I moved to the Buckeye School System in Medina, Ohio. It was the right time to change schools, and of course, I was upfront to the executive team and staff about my basketball endeavors after school hours. I vowed that it would never impact my performance, nor would I miss school because of doing games. They were excited for me and could not possibly have been more supportive.

1975 was going to be my year. New school, a Varsity college rotation, and more games...are you friggin' kidding me? This was getting to be really exciting. And hey, there might even be more than 22 people in the stands.

The MAC is such a great league. I have always thought that the mid-major conferences never got the recognition they deserve. True, you don't have the mega stars playing in this league, but you do have the kids that got to this level based on basketball smarts and playing fundamentally sound. It was a great place to start my Division 1 career.

In that 1975-76 season, Western Michigan, Miami, and Toledo battled all year for conference supremacy with Western Michigan eventually claiming the top spot. I don't recall exactly how many games I officiated that year, but I knew I was performing well and I was having the time of my life doing it. How did I know I was doing well? Feedback from the officiating supervisors and coaches said so…

Now came the offseason in 1976. I was already riding high with my experience in the MAC and couldn't wait to do it again in 1977. Wouldn't you know it; I received another call out of the blue that would eventually shape my life for the next three decades.

"Phil, this is Herm Rohrig, supervisor of officials from The Big 10 Conference. John Payak has spoken very highly of you."

John Payak (left) and Herm Rohrig (seated)

Wow. That came out of nowhere. Herm was actually a retired football player, having played for the Green Bay Packers in the 1940s. After he retired, he worked as a scout and official in the NFL and had the distinct honor of refereeing the very first Super Bowl in 1967. He then moved on to basketball and ultimately became the head of officials for the Big 10.

"We would like you to consider working for the Big 10 beginning in 1976."

The Big 10?? Whoa. I could hear my heart beating outside my chest. The Big 10 was on top of the basketball world in the mid-70s. Bobby Knight and the Indiana Hoosiers just went undefeated the year before and had the entire sports planet buzzing.

Donna and I had some serious conversations. Instead of road trips to Oxford, Ohio and Ypsilanti, Michigan....working games would now include places like Madison, Wisconsin and

Iowa City, Iowa. More time travelling to and from and more time away from home. More pressure. BUT—it was a chance for more money, more prestige, and more games…and the chance to make a name for myself on TV. Move over Kojak, there's another bald eagle coming to town.

What would I do with the MAC? What would I do with the Buckeye school system? I loved both those places AND I was committed to them both. Commitment is a big thing for me and I didn't want to let anyone down.

Screw it. I'm doing all three. At the same time.

I called him back and confirmed, "Mr. Rohrig, I would be honored to work for the Big 10."

Somehow I was able to call the shots a bit in terms of my employment. I committed to a full Big 10 schedule in 1976 with the understanding that my commitment to being an educator at Buckeye was the top priority. Weeknight games would include closer places to home like Columbus, Ann Arbor, and East Lansing, while every school was fair game on the weekends. I then made myself available to the MAC on non-Big 10 days…as places like Kent, Toledo and Akron were easy to get to on school nights. Through it all, I made sure I was home in time to answer the bell for school the next morning. It was a hectic plan, and honestly, I'm not sure how I sold it to Donna, because it would be a great burden on her. She was all-in, and supported me 100%. With her and the kids on board, I knew I could do it.

Suddenly the 1976 season was upon us. It was time to put my plan of attack in motion. I started to work some non-conference games for the MAC and the Big 10. In the Big 10, it was a great way to get my feet wet in the new conference as the big boys usually scheduled Northwest Cupcake State and Meatball

University. These games were generally blowouts, where one call or another wasn't going to affect the outcome of the game. I did the normal slate and anxiously looked forward to my first conference game in the Big 10. I wondered who I'd get? I knew the DATE of the game but didn't necessarily know the game or venue yet. I was the new guy, so I assumed I would get a couple of the cellar dwellers to kick things off.

Nope.

January 6, 1977. Assembly Hall in Bloomington, Indiana. Purdue at Indiana. Not only did I get the defending champions, I got the legendary Coach Knight with one of his fiercest rivals

Good Lord.

On the day of the game, I stayed with my typical routine, trying to keep everything as normal as possible. Did I have butterflies? You bet your bottom dollar I did.

I walked into a restroom at Indiana, and I must have looked nervous. In the restroom, a woman walked up to me and asked if I was the official for the game, and if I was nervous.

"Yes, I am doing the game, and no, I'm not nervous…"

She looked at me with a crooked smile and asked,

"Well, why are you in the women's restroom?"

Ugh.

I quickly collected myself and headed toward the locker room that I actually belonged in. I had to get my head straight and prepare for the game. I wondered who I would be working with. Already in the locker room was the legendary Charlie Fouty.

Charlie was extremely well respected in the business. He was a tough talking, cigar chomping, gravelly voiced presence. Fouty had been on the hardwood doing high school games as early as 1948 and was in the twilight of his hoops career. He had just done the Final Four the previous season, and he didn't take any crap from coaches. He also had a way of working peacefully with Coach Knight. I'm sure it's no accident that Fouty was placed in this Big 10 opener with the reigning champs. How I got there…I have no idea!

I didn't say too much before the game. I was in the midst of officiating royalty, so I kept my mouth shut and mentally prepared myself for the ballgame. Bobby Knight. Assembly Hall. Defending champs. Big 10 Opener. Rivalry game. 17,000 screaming lunatics in the stands. Working with the great Charlie Fouty. This was the big time.

We were on the floor just minutes before tip-off. Charlie knew about me being a rookie and that this was really my first taste of big time college basketball. I was sure that he would give me some words of wisdom before the game. He had been through hundreds of games and scores of marquis matchups. He had already done three Final Fours. I couldn't wait to see what this wealth of knowledge…this wizard on the hardwood was going to tell me. The horn sounded. The teams were about to take the floor. Charlie then approached me. Finally. Can't wait to see what he has to say.

"Hey, Bova," in his jagged glass gargling voice.

"Yeah, Charlie…?"

"Don't fuck it up."

Welcome to the Big 10.

23

Purdue put the wood to the Hoosiers that night in a convincing 80-63 win. Coach Knight was his usual self, obviously frustrated at the results of the game and the way the season had started after coming off the undefeated campaign. Charlie was his masterful self that night. Coach Knight always had affection for General Patton, and Charlie was LIKE a little general out there—in complete control of the game. Maybe that's why Coach Knight had a friendship with Charlie. He knew the game was in good hands and that Charlie was the authoritative and undisputed general out there. My take away from that night was the way that he carried himself on the floor and how I could model my budding career in a way that coaches would respect what I did. My effort and commitment to getting things right, while pleasing those that I was working for was always there. How else do you gain respect? How else do you earn the trust and respect of the most difficult coaches in the game? Well, now it was clear. Work your ass off and follow in the words of the immortal Charlie Fouty:

"Don't fuck it up."

"You can say something to popes, kings and presidents but you can't talk to refs. In the next war, they ought to give everyone a whistle."

-Abe Lemons

2

<u>Referee 101</u>

I thought I might mention a little about the nuts and bolts of being a referee before continuing on with some of the stories, situations and personalities that I have been lucky enough to experience.

The art of officiating a ball game is much more difficult than it seems from the stands. Of course, you need to know all the rules like the back of your hand, the placement of the inbound, and the administration of the shot clock. It goes on and on. Just as difficult, an excellent official works in concert with his partners, even though he/she may have only met them for the first time in pregame. Tough to know tendencies of your partners if you have never worked with them before! Fans don't care about that, players don't care about that, and coaches certainly don't give a rat's behind either. The anticipation and EXPECTATION is that the officiating crew will work as one, see everything, and not make mistakes. Anything less than perfection will lead to one team saying the 'ref screwed us that time'. I'm here to tell you, the best officials make mistakes every game, and we really don't care who wins.

Even though there is often unfamiliarity with your partners

or potentially the gym that you are working in, there are several things that remain the same in being a college basketball referee: Positioning and Protocol, Per Diem, Game Arrival, and Pregame.

Positioning and Protocol

The high school and college game gets bigger, faster, and stronger seemingly every year. Early on, two officials were assigned to each game, and it eventually changed to the three man game that we see today. There is just too much happening at once and happening so quickly. The way I saw it, six eyes watching is more than four eyes, and that's a good thing.

Very commonly, three people working a game will set up in a triangular formation. One person will set up as the Center, one will be the Lead, and the last person is the Trail. The Center will set up opposite the scorer's table and roam from free throw line extended to free throw line extended. The Lead is the official at the baseline, while the Trail will be on the same side as the scorer's table and set up beyond the 3 point arc.

The Center official is responsible for the opposite half of the lane from where the Lead is set up and everything from the backside lane extended to half court. It's the Center's responsibility to watch all things on the back side of the ball. Holding, rebounding (box outs and player control), and things of that nature are common to this area.

The Lead, who sets up on the baseline, has responsibility within the 3 point arc and his half of the lane, up to the free throw line. The Lead will watch out for off the ball movement and all the physicality underneath. Calls on the baseline, block/charge, and possession calls are what the Lead referee will see often.

And finally, the Trail official is on the same side of the

court as the Lead and watches over the area outside the 3-point line on his side of the floor to the opposite side lane extended, where the Center takes over. The Trail will watch over 3-point attempts, hand checking, and things of that nature that occur outside the arc.

When play transitions to the other side of the floor, the Center can remain foul line extended, while the Trail can become the Lead, and the Lead can take the Trail's position. From there, it's a constant flow back and forth from possession to possession, where each official is running 2/3 of the floor.

By the way, these positions are interchangeable during the course of a game. You aren't assigned to that position and stuck there for the game. As an example, it's common practice for the official calling a foul (and reporting to the scoring table) to take the Center position upon his return to the action. The others will then fill the role of the Lead and Trail. That's just another example of how critical it is that the crew work together and BE a crew.

Even though each ref has a specific area of responsibility, if he sees something outside his area, he calls it…especially if it's something off the ball while his partner ref is watching on the ball. Does it drive coaches nuts when an official calls something from across the floor that his partner didn't see in front of him? Sure does. "How can you see something from 40 feet away when your partner is two feet away?" If I had a nickel every time I heard that…. Either way, if an infraction happens, it should be called. The bottom line for the official is to call the game as best as possible and in the best interest for the teams and the players. Call it like you see it.

What happens when you DON'T see it? What happens when you are at a bad angle or your line of vision is blocked? Good officials will check with their partners and tap their chest asking for help. The partner ref will then point in the right direction and the area official will make the call. Getting it right is better than a guess. The kids playing put too much time and energy into the game for a call to be made on a coin flip. By the same token, if your partner makes a call that is blatantly incorrect, it's OK to step in and correct the situation. Usually, it will be an out of bounds call. There's a fine line between supporting your crewmates and overruling them, but if you overrule, you better be right!

As an authority figure on the floor, you have to portray yourself as in complete control. As important, when making calls, make them with strength and conviction! Blow the whistle, point in the correct direction with power, and yell "BLUE!" That shows authority and confidence. Blowing a whistle half-heartedly and saying, "Um, I think it's Blue's ball" will have you cleaning horse stalls before you know it.

Per Diem

Depending on the conference you are working for, there is a "per diem" amount that is given to you. Sometimes that can be a separate amount on top of the wage you're earning for a game, or it can be a total package number which is inclusive of your wage and your expenses.

A 'per diem' is an allowance given to you for your expenses in travel to the game. Items that are part of your per diem amount can include airfare/travel, hotel, and food. For example, you may be allotted a $500 amount for a game in Evanston, Illinois on a Saturday. You have the ability to use that money as you wish in order to get there by all means necessary. Could that be a flight in and out on the same day? Sure. Could it mean driving up the night before and staying a night or two in a hotel? Absolutely. Eating steak or eating McDonald's…your choice. Some guys will spend every last nickel of their per diem in order to make the journey as 'luxurious' as possible, while others will do it on the cheap and pocket the extra. Personal preference, I suppose. For me, leftover hot dogs and boxes of popcorn usually did the trick on late night drives back home!

Game Arrival

The general rule of thumb is that officials should be in the locker room at least 90 minutes before game time to start preparing to work the game. If a game was scheduled during the week in the evening, it was OK to arrive to the host school prior to that 90 minute window. If the game was scheduled PRIOR to 3 pm on a weekend, it was expected that the official arrive in town the night before. That would help eliminate possible travel/weather issues and delays. That way, the world could come to an end prior to a nooner on Saturday, and you would already be in town ready for action.

For me, I didn't like to rush and tried to arrive comfortably, so I set my goal to be there two hours prior to tip time. This rule worked OK for me, as I could work at Buckeye until the end of the day, and then hop in the car and head out to the MAC or Big 10 school I was working. If I had to do a game at State College or West Lafayette on the weekend, I could take off the night before— or morning, depending on game time—and still be back in town to meet my students on that Monday morning.

Pregame

After the officials arrive 90 minutes before the game and prepare to work, the crew will have a "Pregame" meeting in advance of the ball game they are about to work. This usually happens somewhere between 45 and 60 minutes prior to tip off time.

During the meeting, the crew would discuss a number of things. Most importantly, what to do if something occurs out of the ordinary. How do we react? What do we do? Who does what? Most college hoops fans know I had an incident with a chair that I will get into later, but no matter the situation, the folks in stripes need to be in command. We just need to be on the same page in order to do it.

Besides preparation for all things unknown, we would also compare some notes about the teams and coaches in the ball game. Did certain players have reputations for things that we needed to watch for? Was there a past incident between these two teams that would cause us to be on high alert for any shenanigans? Were the coaches known for behaving poorly, stepping outside the coaching box, or other causes for concern? The more the crew was prepared for what we were about to take on, the better chance for a well officiated contest. And in reality, that's all that anyone really wants.

Before we move on...you want to laugh? From time to time, officials will have a "double whistle" on a foul, as they may see things differently. This happens most often on the block/charge call, which we refer to as a "blarge" (half block, half charge).

Needless to say, it takes two officials for the 'blarge' to occur. It shouldn't happen in a game, but unfortunately, it sometimes does. Coaches aren't happy when officials aren't on the same page. Players aren't either, as they are both assessed personal fouls, and we determine possession based on the arrow at the scorer's table.

Well, in my first year on a Big Ten crew, I had my OWN personal blarge! How is that possible when you need a block and a charge to be called at the same time?

As an unexperienced official, I got so caught up in the moment that I was yelling "CHARGE", but showed the signal for a block.

Both my partners came up to me and looked at me as if I was Jack Nicholson in "One Flew Over the Cuckoo's Nest". My one partner asked if I was OK. In that moment, I had no idea why he was asking.

"Phil, we just had a blarge and you are the ONLY guy that blew the whistle!"

Ugh. I wish I had a video of me trying to explain to the coaches what had just transpired. Lesson learned…slow down and don't get caught up in the moment!

Oh well. On to travel….

"I wanted to have a career in sports when I was young but I had to give up the idea. I'm only six feet tall, so I couldn't play basketball. I'm only 190 pounds, so I couldn't play football, and I have 20/20 vision so I couldn't be a referee."

-Jay Leno

3

You Better Make it on Time Even if Your Plane Crashes

I don't think too many people realize the effort involved in scheduling and travel for a season. All the college teams playing big time ball have an Athletic Director and support staff to schedule ball games, travel, equipment, food, etc. Everything necessary to put the kids in the best position to compete and not have to worry about the particulars that accompany travel to and from games is taken care of. For us zebras, that's ALL on us. TGFD. (Thank God For Donna). We handle every last detail to do everything in our power to get to that contest 90 minutes before one of us tosses the ball up in the air.

I can't overemphasize enough how important it is to have a friend, partner, spouse, or what have you to be a support system. Donna helped me tremendously in planning the run around to all the games. My friend Bob Garn would accompany me to many sites so I could take a power nap while in transit. I was very fortunate.

About a month before the season starts, the conference that you are affiliated with will send you a schedule of dates that games are to be played. At that point, you don't see what games you are assigned to, or which venues they are going to be played at...just dates. Once you select the dates you can work, you communicate back to the Supervisor of Officials. In my case, I had to be very careful to compare those dates to certain days of the week that I may have had school conflicts. I wanted to be sure I didn't double book myself, and again, my commitment to the kids and staff at school was my priority. To that end, I made myself available on almost all the weekends to take some of the pressure off of my brother officials.

Now that your dates are selected, you can then look at the available dates for other conferences that you had allegiance to. I still worked the Mid-American regularly, so I would fill dates for games in that league—scheduling around my educator position and the commitment to the Big 10. Several years later, I would add games for the Atlantic 10 and Horizon League, but I will get into that a little more later.

The Supervisor will then start the painstaking task of assigning officials to each of the games. More often than not, those assignments weren't known to the officials until a couple weeks before the game. He would have to juggle veteran officials with rookies, try to make sense of scheduling from a logistical/travel standpoint, assign his top guys for marquis matchups, and things of that nature.

The assignments to games weren't made too far in advance for several reasons. What if an official wasn't performing to the league's expectations? That person certainly should not be rewarded with an over-abundance of games. What if a coach and official have a definite issue with each other? It probably wouldn't make sense to pair those two up a multitude of times. There's enough drama ON the floor...no need to cause drama before the game starts! What if a team that was picked in the bottom of the conference surprises everyone and challenges for the league title? And the opposite? It was the Supervisor's job and responsibility to schedule all those games appropriately.

That all sounds like it makes good sense, right? It sure does—unless of course you are the official that has to scramble with travel arrangements to make those assignments a reality. The entire planet may know that Ohio State is playing Michigan in Columbus on January 27, but I may not know I am doing the game until January 13. Needless to say, that scramble to make sure I was where I was supposed to be was sometimes challenging. Not only did I have to get my travel scheduled, I also had three kids with their own schedules but so did everyone in my family. Rides to practice, to friend's houses, to the doctor…all those things were very important as well. That's where TGFD comes in. Without Donna's ability to be a master scheduler, travel agent, taxi driver, and all-around great mom, I don't know how I would have done it.

Anyway, once the dates are established and eventually the arenas, it became imperative to schedule my travel time as best as possible. I didn't have too much "time sensitive" pressure on weekends, so I could fly to games comfortably and not have to worry about being back at a certain time. Games during the week, however, became more of a challenge. I was getting some pressure to do games that were longer drives and while I wanted to please the Commissioner to stay in good standing and get the plum assignments, I also wanted to be sure the Principal at my school was happy with me as well.

It became typical to have two, three, and four hour drives each way, which was of course after a school day and running up and down the floor in a high pressure situation. Exhausting to be sure. And that's when Bob Garn was so valuable to help out. He was a hoops junkie and loved going to games as well. It was an ideal situation for both of us when he could join in. Driving or not, nights were long, and caffeine of any kind and I were beginning to become best friends.

I remember one night after a game at Penn State, I started the drive back to Cleveland at around 10pm. Normally, that would get me back home around 2am…but this drive was a little different. The snow was coming down in buckets, the roads were icy, and I could only see about as far as Jimmy Jackson's range on his jump shot. The drive was slower than normal…then started to slow to a crawl…and then to a dead stop. In these Alaskan Tundra conditions, there was an 18-wheeler up ahead that jack knifed and blocked all lanes of traffic. I was stuck.

I sat at a dead stop on the Pennsylvania Turnpike for a good long while. I looked at the clock radio on my car and felt more and more drained every time the numbers turned, knowing full well that I still had a hefty drive in front of me, and I still had to be at my best in the morning. Those kids needed me. They depended on me, and I wasn't going to let them down. I thought to myself that what I was doing was nuts. I loved the game and my job, but it wasn't worth killing myself to do it.

To keep a long story somewhat short, I eventually pulled into my driveway around 4am. I was exhausted. Hyped up on bucket loads of coffee, but absolutely drained. Most of us have depended on the Caffeine Gods to get us through the night on occasion, but as you know, sometimes you can't just turn off the caffeine when it's time to put your head on the pillow. I think I slept somewhere between 4 and 6 minutes that night before the alarm clock went off. It was time to get ready for school. Ugh.

I found the biggest mug I owned and poured as much coffee as I could into it. If I could have filled my garbage can up with some java and taken in with me, I would have. It was at that point that I thought espresso through IV might be a good idea. I trudged back to the car that was still warm from having just turned it off a short while ago and headed to Buckeye High School.

I arrived at school, and sure enough, the first person I bumped into was the school's principal, Dave Kuhn. Dave was a great guy, and I enjoyed working with him. As much as I tried to hide how exhausted I was, my blood shot eyes were a dead giveaway.

"Mornin' Phil. Rough night?"

I'm pretty sure I replied with something that didn't sound like anything that resembled words from the English language.

"Phil, come into my office for a minute," he said.

We took the walk down the hall and headed for his office. Whether you are in kindergarten or a grown adult, no one likes to get called down to the principal's office. I was too tired to even try and figure out if we had stuff to talk about, or if I was in trouble. The game was on TV the evening before, so I'm pretty sure he knew why I looked the way I did. He knew I was in State College the night before.

He started, "My son is learning to become a pilot."

I exhaled under my breath. At this point, I felt pretty sure that I wasn't going to get swatted, or that I had to wait for him to call my mother and explain to her why I was sitting in this office.

"Craig has been in the air a number of times and is looking to get his hours. He can rent planes at the Lorain County Airport. Rent the plane for him, buy his gas, and give him a few bucks for his time…and maybe this will help solve your weekday travel

36

problem. He gets his hours in the air; you get to your games on time and back to school safely."

Hmmm, very interesting. I could do State College or West Lafayette in one quarter of the time and still be in bed by a decent hour.

"Please give Craig my phone number," I told him.

I don't know this guy from a bale of hay, but man, if I can master this travel plan, my life would get 10 times easier. And so would Donna's, which was equally important.

As luck would have it, I was scheduled for Penn State a couple weeks later. I decided to take Principal Kuhn's advice and contacted Craig. We made the necessary arrangements for our inaugural flight together. I left school after the final bell, picked up trusty Bob Garn to travel with me, and ventured to Lorain County Airport to meet Craig. The airport was about 35 minutes from the High School. This was going to be great!

I parked my car and went inside to the tiny terminal. Craig was seated, but must have known who I was, and stood to greet me.

"Mr Bova, I'm Craig Kuhn, I will be your pilot."

Craig "The Mantis" Kuhn

As a basketball official, I was used to being around a lot of large individuals. When this dude stood up, he dwarfed me. Skinny as a rail, and easily had to be 6 foot 7. Arms and legs everywhere. Not sure he actually had a body. He looked every bit like a Praying Mantis. I looked at him and then looked at the tiny airplane…a miniscule Piper II aircraft that fit four people on a good day.

"Um, Craig, are you going to fit in that thing?" I asked.

"No worries, sir. I fly all the time. You have a ball game to get to," he replied.

"OK. Let's go."

Good Lord, not like I have any other options, right?

Bob and I climbed into the plane and so did Craig. We taxied down the runway, picked up speed and headed into the sky for the short flight to State College. Instead of 4+ hours by car, we should touch down in 45 minutes.

Before I knew it, we started to descend. Craig was
handling the plane like a seasoned veteran. He yelled over to me
that we were about to land, so I tightened up the seatbelt and
started to think about the ball game. The wheels came down and
touched the runway.

When I tell you this was the roughest, bumpiest runway I
had ever been on, I'm telling the God's honest truth. It was just as
gravelly as Fouty's voice. After bracing myself, I looked out the
window and noticed that they hadn't even cleared the snow from
the runway! I knew we were coming into a small Regional
Airport, but to not even have the runway plowed was extremely
odd to me. I looked back at Bob, and he gave me a shrug…as if he
had the answer to why we landed in snow.

Craig finally brought the tiny plane to a halt and wasn't
exactly sure where to go. This airport was dark and it didn't even
seem like there was anyone there. I know he had mentioned to me
that we would be coming into University Park Airport, but I
couldn't even see a sign for it.

We all started looking out the window trying to determine
which way to go. When I tell you this joint was dead, I'm talking
about no-signs-of -life anywhere dead. In the distance we finally
saw some headlights, and the car started to head our way. Great, I
thought, this must be our ride to the terminal.

Nope.

"Who the hell are you?" barked the guy in military attire.

My pilot went dead silent. I guess I had to speak up. I've
never done the private plane thing before, so I wasn't sure if this

was the protocol or not.

"Phil Bova. I have the Penn State game tonight."

The guy in fatigues didn't seem too impressed. He clenched his jaw and had the most irritated look on his face. More irritated than Gene Keady after getting T'd up.

"You landed in a military airport. You did not have permission to land here. You have 5 minutes to turn this plane around and get the hell out of here. I strongly suggest leaving immediately before I stick your asses in jail."

He didn't have to ask twice. Craig quickly morphed into "The Mantis" nickname I gave him, seemingly grew an extra couple of appendages, and started flicking every lever he had to get us out of there. We went back down that uneven runway that probably hasn't been used since the Lincoln administration and got out of there.

It turns out we landed at Mid-State Airport in Phillipsburg, PA. I'm guessing it was somewhere near the State College, but I had no idea. All I know is that I felt lucky that we weren't shot down by America's finest.

"Um, Craig, what happened?"

"I'm a pilot, not a road map."

Perfect.

My directionally challenged pilot eventually got us to the right airport, and I scrambled to get to the Bryce Jordan Center as quickly as possible. I ended up taking the floor minutes before the National Anthem and got the *Malocchio* from my partners who thought I had stiffed them.

"Phil, where have you been???"

"I could tell you, but you'd NEVER believe me in a hundred years."

Oh yeah and then there was the time in 1996. Tuesday, January 30, 1996, to be exact. That's one of those dates that The Mantis and I won't forget. Sure enough, I had Bob come with me as he enjoyed traveling to the games that I worked.

I had the Iowa/Indiana game in Indiana and as I mentioned, it was during the week. Despite my rough debut with The Mantis...uhh...Craig, we decided to take to the skies and head to Bloomington. To travel an hour in the sky vs five hours in the car seemed like a good idea.

I picked up Bob and we met Craig at the Lorain Airport and took off smoothly. We were ahead of schedule, it was a beautiful day, and all was going perfectly. The flight touched down at about 4:30—at the CORRECT AIRPORT this time. I looked out the window, and the snow started coming. It was snowing like you wouldn't believe. After touching down, Craig tried to find an empty hangar to help it survive the Arctic weather. Unfortunately nothing was available, so we had to let it the plane sit unprotected from the elements.

The three of us made it to the game on time, and it was a beauty. Nip and tuck the whole game. It was a tight contest right to the end. Every possession was valuable with time outs being used like crazy. It was a great game that Indiana eventually won 76-73, but a LONG game.

I hit the showers, had the postgame conference with the

Referee Observer that was there to watch. We pulled out of Assembly Hall and headed toward the airport around 11pm. At this point, there had to have been 6-8 inches on the ground and it was bitter cold. The wind was howling and the conditions were just flat out miserable.

The guys at the airport helped prep the plane. I had coffee in hand, and I'm ready to head out. It's been a long day, and I have Michigan State at the Breslin Center the next night. I'm ready to get a few minutes of sleep while in the air.

Craig gets in, tries to fire up the plane and is clearly having some difficulty. You know that sound that your lawnmower makes when it won't kick in? It's that same sound that the motor makes when it is crying for mercy. Yep, that was my plane.

"We have a problem, Mr. Bova," Craig says.

"Fix the friggin' problem, Craig."

Bob and I went back in for yet another cup of coffee.

A half hour later, Craig comes back in and announces we are good to go. I follow him to the plane, we buckle in, he puts the headset on, and we start toward the runway. He picked up speed, pulled on the throttle and says that something doesn't feel right.

"Mr. Bova, we have another problem," he says.

"Fix the friggin' problem, Craig," I say again.

He turns the plane around, we head back to the gate, and I head in for the obligatory cup o' joe refill. My eyeballs are swimming in coffee at this point. Screw it, I added a doughnut for good measure. Seemed like a good idea.

Now it's close to 1am. Craig came in and says the following:

"Mr Bova, we will be good to go shortly. I have to give the plane a blow first."

I looked at Bob. Bob looked at me. We looked at each other not quite sure what to say. It was the same look you would expect to see if someone asked you to solve some Chinese Algebra.

"Ummmmm…what?" Bob asked.

Now, I'm curious. I have no idea where this is headed, but just as sure as the day is long, I am interested to find out. I can't help myself but to ask:

"You must reeeeeally like flying, don't you, Craig?"

At this point all three of us are staring at each other like The Three Stooges. Craig closed his eyes slowly and shook his head realizing the confusion.

"A TORPEDO BLOW. Since the plane has frozen over, we need to open the hood and use a torpedo heater to blow hot air in and thaw all the components…you know, make sure nothing is iced up. That was the problem."

Thank God. How in the world was I going to explain to his father that his son Craig was a nut job?

After The Mantis blew the plane (with the torpedo blower!), he came in and assured us we are finally ready to go. We headed back to the tin can that we are about to head home in.

"I think we are finally good," he tells us.

I think he was trying to convince himself more than he was trying to convince us. After all, I can sleep once we get up there. He still has to get this thing landed and preferably at the right airport.

"Are you sure this time? No propeller stroking or wing caressing needed?" I asked mockingly.

He mumbled something under his breath that was probably a good thing that I didn't hear it.

We head down the runway and this thing is making noises I have never heard come out of a plane. Craig picks up speed and begins to lift up. I think we got as high as 12 feet before the plane lost power. I didn't take Airplane Physics 101, but I was pretty sure that wasn't supposed to happen.

Our tin can maintained 12 feet for a few seconds, but without power, it sure as heck wasn't going higher. It started to descend and eventually landed on the runway. Hard. We were sliding all over the place. Sparks were flying. Bob was hanging on-to one of my arms, I had a death grip on the arm rest, while our pilot kept his paws at 10 and 2 on the wheel—determined to not let us veer off the runway. How do you steer something in these conditions? No idea. But he was trying. And doing a great job.

It finally came to a stop. We knew sparks were flying so we had to get out as soon as possible. Bob somehow shimmied down to safety. I did some sort of dismount that would have made Mary Lou Retton proud. The Mantis used his cricket-like ability to spring out of the seat. We then took off running not knowing if this thing was going to blow. A fire truck passed us and went to the site of our plane. They hosed it down before things escalated.

We were petrified as we got to the terminal.

Forget the coffee. Give me a bottle of bourbon. I love basketball…but really!?! The three of us hugged each other like we had just cut down the nets at the Final Four.

That's all well and good, but now it's 2 am and I still have Sparty in East Lansing in about 18 hours. Now what am I supposed to do?

The only shot we had was to head toward Indianapolis and to catch a plane the next morning toward Cleveland. I snagged a car and made the hour trip with the guys up 37 North toward Indianapolis. Luckily, there was a Holiday Inn within shouting distance of the airport. We checked in and got about 14 minutes of sleep. Craig dragged Bob and I to Indianapolis International, while he took off back to Bloomington to figure out the status of the plane he had rented.

Lost in all this craze was the fact that I had school the next day. Aye yi yi. It just wasn't possible for me to get there. I couldn't call in sick, because half the planet saw me on ESPN in Bloomington the night before. I came clean. I had too much respect for Mr. Kuhn to lie. I did have one thing going for me…he helped create The Mantis, so there may be some sympathy there.

I called and he could not have possibly been more understanding. He told me he would take care of me, and more importantly, for his son and me to make it back in one piece.

"Thank God you are alive. Don't worry about school. If this doesn't qualify as an Emergency Day, I don't know what does. Tell Craig I am not paying for the plane you guys blew up."

"I owe you one, Dave," I replied.

One less thing to worry about.

There was a flight to Cleveland fairly early, so I used up all my per diem in a last minute fare and got back home. Donna waited for our arrival (TGFD) and we tried to figure out which way was up. My car was in Lorain. Since I just flew in commercial, she picked us up at Cleveland Hopkins.

We picked up the car in Lorain and headed back home. I had to get at least a few minutes of sleep. It was already past noon, and Michigan State was tipping off against #10 Penn State at 7pm. I still had a 4 hour drive ahead of me and had to be in the locker room by 5:30.

Since my cahones were still in my throat from the night before, there was no way in the world I was going to fly. I had a better chance of getting hit by lightning, twice, before I was going to get back in a puddle jumper.

I made Bob go with me so we could take turns driving and sleeping. We made it to East Lansing on time and saw a real barn burner. Michigan State squeaked out a 61-58 winner.

The ball game ended, I cleaned up, did the review with the observer, and got back on the road around 10pm. During that four hour drive, Bob and I kept replaying the night before, realizing that we were fortunate to even be alive. I'm sure that's what kept us up.

Next thing I know, it's 2am and I am pulling into my driveway. Now it's Thursday, February 1. I have to be at school in about 5 hours. Since Praying Mantis, Sr. got me off the hook the night before, I sure as heck wasn't going to push my luck. I ended up welcoming my students to class that morning

46

That day was the last time I ever flew on a single engine plane. Since that day, I arrived to games by car or by commercial airline.

I always had the utmost respect for Craig and his ability as a pilot. Flying to as many games as we had, I felt very safe with him. He was thorough and had safety as his first priority. Great job, Craig!

By the way, in case you are wondering, The Mantis is NOT your commercial pilot flying you to your next vacation destination. He took a different path in life and now works for the railroad!

"Hey Ref...you might want to check your phone, you have missed quite a few calls."

-Penn State Fan

4

Top 10 Arenas

Speaking of travelling, let's take it a step further with my favorite places I have been fortunate enough to work. I do love the Big 10, but have been assigned to work a number of different places around the country for tournaments or non-conference games. Because of the regionality of assigning officials, I very rarely did games west of the Mississippi. Needless to say, I was never able to do any games in such iconic places as Pauley Pavilion at UCLA or Allen Fieldhouse in Kansas. Still, there are dozens of outstanding basketball arenas on this side of the country.

For the sake of my Top 10 list, I will exclude the pro venues. As we all know, those are gazillion dollar facilities that are financed by the money machine that is the NBA. As beautiful as those places are, they don't have the same atmosphere as venues that are strictly for the college game. They are built for the corporate and luxury suite world, rather than the 19 and 20 year olds that dip themselves in paint before coming to a game.

But if you ARE curious, the 3 professional arenas that I enjoyed working in most were Gund Arena (now Rocket Mortgage FieldHouse) in Cleveland, Conseco Fieldhouse in Indianapolis, and Madison Square Garden in New York City.

I guess it goes without saying why The Gund makes the list. As a Cleveland boy, it really was an honor to officiate games in the best arena in town. At the time the Gund was built (coinciding with Jacobs Field…now Progressive Field for the Indians), it was state of the art. The Cavaliers played in the old Richfield Coliseum for several years, and Gund Arena was a by-product of the movement to upgrade Cleveland sports facilities. The Mid-American Conference moved their tournament there and I absolutely loved doing those games. Plus I could get home and to bed 30 minutes after leaving the arena!

Conseco Fieldhouse (now Banker's Life Fieldhouse) opened in 1999 to replace the old Market Square Arena in downtown Indianapolis. In 2005 and 2006, Conseco was named as the #1 arena in the NBA by the Sports Business Journal, and I'm not surprised. It has a beautiful glass façade on the outside and sprawling atrium on the inside—while sitting in the middle of downtown Indy. The Big 10 alternates doing their tournament here and in Chicago, and it was an excellent choice. Gorgeous facility for basketball.

Finally, how can you mention basketball and not mention Madison Square Garden? MSG was built in the 60s and remains one of the few professional arenas not named after a corporation. Can you imagine the cost of the naming rights for that place?? The Garden just drips with history—everything from basketball to concerts to boxing. You name it, The Garden has hosted it. Let's be honest, the arena itself isn't the most sparkling thing out there, but it's located in the heart of Manhattan and that alone gives the place some extra juice. It's not known as the "Mecca of Basketball" for nothing. Certainly a bucket list place for any real sports fan.

OK, enough of the pros. Let's get back to the college side

where fans trade tickets for kegs of beer and where kids wear speedos to games for that chance to be on TV. Mom and Dad must be so proud at home…

Here's my personal Top 10 list of places that I have officiated games.

10. The Palestra, Philadelphia, PA

The Palestra is actually home to the Penn Quakers of the Ivy League, but it is much more iconic than that. It opened in 1927 and was one of the largest arenas in the world at the time, and it's one of the first to be built from steel and concrete. Holding roughly 10,000 fans, The Palestra is often known as "the birthplace of college basketball."

The Big 5 Philadelphia teams (LaSalle, Penn, St Joseph, Temple, and Villanova) originally played their home games there before moving to other arenas, and they still occasionally play each other there in their intra-city battles. In total, The Palestra has hosted more college basketball games and more visiting teams than any other gym in the country. In 2007, ESPN did a documentary called "The Palestra: Cathedral of College Basketball." It was titled correctly.

The other thing The Palestra was famous for was that fans were so close to the game. REALLY close. Almost uncomfortably close. The first row of the bleachers actually touched the floor. There was no barrier between the fans and the playing court. Along the sides, fans were right on top of you, very similar to a high school gym.

Now, try calling a game in that situation. It was

smothering…but FANTASTIC. I'm sure people in the front rows could see what color gum I was chewing, just as I could hear a couple argue over post game plans.

If you had two Big 5 teams playing each other, that was a tough ticket with all the alumni in the Philadelphia area. You can bet your last nickel that fans would be fired up for those games. If one of the Big 5 was playing a team from out of town, that joint was rocking from beginning to end.

In the era of high end palaces and corporate dollars, The Palestra remains a gem.

9. The Carrier Dome, Syracuse, NY

On the complete opposite end of the spectrum from the fabulous Palestra is the Carrier Dome at Syracuse. The dome hosts football and basketball for the Orange and holds just under 50,000 folks. It's the only dome in the Northeast and only arena of its kind on a college campus. They shrink capacity for college hoops to around 33,000, but the Carrier Dome routinely leads the nation in attendance per game/per season.

While Jim Boeheim has done a tremendous job building the basketball program, I believe the Carrier Dome has helped coerce kids to come to Syracuse. It surely helps to recruit a kid when you can tell him that he will be playing in front of the most people in the country!

I have heard the Dome nicknamed as "The Loud House", and they aren't kidding. The inflatable roof allows sound to echo, and packing that many people in for a basketball game helps the cause as well. It was very rare for me to do a game in such a large

51

facility like that one. It was different—tons of people and very
high ceilings. Because of this capacity, the Carrier Dome has
hosted a number of NCAA tournament games. It's a perfect fit for
a basketball crazy town like Syracuse.

Here's one thing that I thought was odd. The Dome had its
naming rights purchased by "Carrier", which of course is a world
leader in heating, air conditioning, and refrigeration products. Can
you guess what the Dome DOESN'T have? Yep. Air
conditioning. I had to make sure there was plenty of water on hand
when the " 'Cuse" was flying up and down the court.

8. Bryce Jordan Center, State College, PA

I won't get into it too much since I mentioned it earlier, but
I really liked coming to this place. Built in the mid-1990s, the
arena has an excellent sound system, electronics, and a great look
to it. The video scoreboard is high quality, and every seat has full
back and arm rests. Not a single bleacher seat in the place.

Overall, Bryce Jordan had a real classy look to it. It was
almost a pro style arena, but enough character to give it a college
atmosphere. Bryce Jordan and Beaver Stadium for football give
Penn State one of the best 1-2 punches for campus venues in the
country.

7. Carmichael Auditorium, Chapel Hill, NC

Prior to the spacious and sprawling Dean Smith Center, the
Tar Heels played their home games in front of 10,000 fans at the
old Carmichael Auditorium. When Carmichael was packed—and
it always was—it was among the loudest I have been in. The gym

had a low roof and students surrounded the court, so to say that it was deafening was an understatement. According to Adam Powell in his book *University of North Carolina Basketball*, Virginia played at Carmichael as the #2 team in the country in 1982, and they couldn't even hear their names being announced prior to the game for the starting lineups. That doesn't surprise me one bit.

There was a real aura about that place. I'm not sure if it was all the history, or all that Carolina blue everywhere, or even the silhouette of the state of North Carolina at the half court line. But man, what a place that was. Dean Smith coached all 20 seasons at Carmichael and left with a 169-20 record. I wasn't a math major, but 20 home losses in 20 years equates to an average of 1 home loss per season. Incredible. It's no wonder they named the next building after him.

I honestly don't recall what game I had at Carmichael in the 80s, but I do remember a kid they had that was pretty good named Jordan. I wonder whatever happened to that guy.

6. Rupp Arena, Lexington, KY

It goes without saying that Rupp Arena and Kentucky basketball are on the short list when talking about storied programs in college basketball. Rupp holds over 23,000 wackos and is the largest basketball-only venue in the country. Rupp is attached to a convention center and shopping area, which makes it even more unique.

Similar to Chapel Hill, Rupp offers a tremendous home court advantage to the Wildcats. Big Blue Nation is well known for their support and following of Kentucky Basketball. At last look, Kentucky historically has won 90% of its home games inside

Rupp. The history speaks for itself, let alone the thousands of fans that bleed Kentucky blue.

The only game I had at Rupp was in December 1985, featuring Denny Crum and #15 ranked Louisville taking on Eddie Sutton's Wildcats, who were #13 in the country. Even the mildest of college basketball fans know fierce rivalry between the Cardinals and the Wildcats. Along with Duke and North Carolina, Louisville and Kentucky are near the top of the list of hated rivals.

While I won't go through all the details of the game, Rupp was absolutely electric. This game was about as high energy of a game that I can recall working.

Behind 23 from Winston Bennett, Kentucky outlasted the 19 point effort from Milt Wagner and won 69-64. Louisville had a hot shot freshman that year named Pervis Ellison who was held to 13 points.

Later that season the Cards got the last laugh as "Never Nervous" Pervis Ellison led the Cardinals to the NCAA Championship beating Duke 72-69. Ellison had 25 and was named the tournament's Most Outstanding Player.

5. Cameron Indoor Stadium, Durham, NC

Speaking of Duke, you want to talk about a crazy atmosphere? Look no further than Cameron Indoor at Duke... This place looks like it could be a chapel from the outside, which is pretty ironic when you think about everyone coming in to worship the Devils.

Even though Cameron was built in 1940, the place is immaculate. You would never think it's as old as it is. It is beautifully preserved, it is truly a shrine to Duke Basketball. Watching on TV, you wouldn't think it is as small as it is. Cameron only holds roughly 9,000 people which is why the Cameron experience is as intimate as it is.

Because it is so small, and Duke is always at the top of the rankings, it's one of the toughest tickets in all of college hoops. Those that are fortunate enough to get in, definitely get their money's worth. The student section is legendary—the Cameron Crazies—and are among the most creative in the land. Some of America's finest attend Duke and definitely do their homework on razzing opposing teams and officials in order to give the home team an added advantage.

I've done games in Cameron twice. Everyone knows how exclusive a school Duke is. The best and the brightest come here to further their education. Both times I did games at Cameron and looked into the student section and wondered what the student in the blue speedo would be in a few years...or how maybe the female painted in blue with horns coming out of her head and devil tail might cure cancer someday. If someone from outer space came to town and was told that the "Crazies" were the future of America, by looks, the alien would say we were doomed. Hard to argue I guess.

Duke's teams over the last few decades have been legendary. Oddly enough, Duke was 0-2 in games I did at Cameron. No particular reason why, just one of those odd statistical quirks that raise their ugly head once in a while. As an example, the Devils were something like 279-29 at home from 1990-2009.

One of those rare home losses occurred on December 2, 1995. Lou Henson brought the Illini to Cameron to take on the

Dukies. Coming in to the game, Duke had won 95 straight home games against non-conference opponents. On that particular day, the Illini outplayed the Blue Devils and came away with a 75-65 win. Yes, yours truly was on the floor doing that game. Needless to say, I wasn't the most popular guy on that side of Tobacco Road.

4. Hinkle Fieldhouse, Butler, IN

Just like the Palestra in Philadelphia, Hinkle Fieldhouse is a must visit destination for any basketball fan. When Hinkle was built in 1928, it was the largest basketball arena in the country. In fact, the United States has named Hinkle a National Historical Landmark in 1987.

This is another place that just oozes history. Hinkle has hosted numerous Indiana High School games and playoffs, presidential visits, all star games, ice capades, and nearly anything else you can think of that would fit in that size of an arena.

The game that Hinkle is probably most known for is the "Milan Miracle" in 1954. (I know what you are thinking...NO...I did NOT do that game.) Before the separation of school size into divisions, all Indiana High School teams competed for ONE state title. That year, tiny Milan High defeated giant Muncie Central for the state championship. Decades later, the basketball film *Hoosiers* was based on that game. And, it was filmed in Hinkle.

The place itself is just full of character. When I officiated games there, I felt like I was part of something bigger. The state of Indiana has always been well known for its love for the game, and Hinkle just felt like hallowed ground. The folks at Butler are very proud of their facility and are very knowledgeable about the game and its roots. I enjoyed working with people that had as much respect for the game as I did, and the Butler faithful are near the top of the list in that regard.

3. Mackey Arena, West Lafayette, IN

As I mention in the chapter about Big 10 arenas, Mackey was a great place to watch a ball game. The Black and Old Gold décor gave the place an intimidating look. Of course you had Purdue Pete—the boilermaker himself—roaming the arena carrying a sledgehammer and keeping the fans engaged. I've often wondered if Purdue Pete and Gene Keady were separated at birth. If you squint a little, those two guys kind of look alike.

The fans are great. Obnoxious and loud. And again, that aluminum roof made the joint a little noisier than if it was of normal construction. From my perspective, the Purdue supporters were relentless on the officials. Why would that make it one of my favorite places to do a game? Simple. I knew I was in for a challenge that night. I had to be at my absolute best, or those eagle-eye fans would let me have it even more than they already were.

On top of all that, Coach Keady was great. There were a few times that he said some things that he probably shouldn't have said to me. I'd walk over and say, "Guess what, Coach?" And he'd yell back in that raspy voice, "I KNOW….I KNOW!" Boom. Technical. And then the place would go nuts. I know he wanted to get T'd up on purpose at times to fire the whole building up, and I was glad to oblige. Of course that made me the bad guy in front of 14,000, but hey, they'll get over it.

Add to all the above that Purdue always had good teams

and that you knew you were in for some good basketball. It's no surprise that Mackey made my list. I always enjoyed that place and all that it brought to the college basketball experience.

2. Joyce Center, South Bend, IN

They say the state of Indiana takes basketball seriously, and looking at my list, the Joyce Center makes the third Indiana venue in my Top 5. The Joyce Center at Notre Dame is situated right next to historic Notre Dame Stadium, and while it doesn't enjoy the same litany of history that the football counterpart does, it has plenty of its own.

Built in 1968 and originally holding 11,000 people, the Joyce Center has had its fair share of big ball games. The Irish handed UCLA their last loss before the 88 game win streak, and then beat them again to end the streak. From 1977-1987, three #1 teams in the country came to town to take on the Irish and left South Bend with a loss and a drop in the rankings. That of course prompted the saying, "Nobody leaves Notre Dame as #1."

I loved coming here. I mean, it's friggin' Notre Dame. You have the familiar fight song....the dancing leprechaun....Digger Phelps with the green carnation...what a great scene. The Shamrocks always play a tough schedule, but the place was always especially electric when DePaul, UCLA, or any of the Big 10 neighbors come to town. There's one game especially that I did with Michigan that stood out for me that I will tell you about later.

Whether football or basketball, love 'em or hate 'em, the Notre Dame experience is a must-do for any college sports fan. That place has a certain mystique about it that is unlike any other.

Don't worry, Officer; I will keep an eye on her....

1. Schottenstein Center, Columbus, OH

O-H-I-O! The Schott didn't have the most character, or the craziest fan base, but it was my favorite place to officiate a game. I will fully admit that there may be a little bias toward enjoying Columbus because I'm an Ohio guy! And of course, it was the shortest ride from my home, so that helped the cause too.

The arena was about as close to a professional arena as any in the country. That's the beauty of college basketball—you have schools playing in palaces like this one, and then you have schools that are playing in gyms that were seemingly built during the Lincoln administration.

In the Big 10, every game is a grind, especially when typical heavyweights like Michigan State, Indiana, and Purdue came to town. While there wasn't as much oomph as when the football counterparts came to town, the game against the school up north always got the crowd's juices flowing a little quicker. The Buckeyes had some excellent players, teams, and seasons, making it a pleasure to take that ride down I-71 toward Columbus.

There were so many fabulous places that I was fortunate enough to do games. The Breslin Center at Michigan State and Assembly Hall at Indiana deserve serious honorable mention considerations. Many of these historic venues are what make college basketball so great. Compare college arenas to their big brothers in the NBA, and you will find that there is SO much more character and history at the college level. Besides Madison Square Garden in Manhattan, what other pro arenas can be considered iconic?

Many of the NBA arenas change names so often that you aren't even sure if the new name arena is the same as the previous one…or one that's brand new!?! Those places are named after airlines, financial companies, banks, and the like. Blah. Boring. Who cares? On campus, these mini hardwood cathedrals may be 50-60-70 years old and named after the athletic director in the 1950s or the guy who nailed the peach basket to the wall for the first time.

Give me that over Corporate America any day of the week. Give me dripping history and ghosts of alumni past as opposed to mega loges and $50 to park. To quote my friend, Mr. Vitale:

"College Basketball is Awesome with a Capital A!"

"The trouble with officials is that they just don't care who wins."

-Tommy Canterbury

5

The Bova Camp—Best in the Country

As I mentioned earlier, I was always a big fan of all sports. Sports have always played a large role in my life, and they have been so good to me. To that point, I have often said that if I ever had the chance to give back in some way, I would welcome the opportunity to do so.

In 1980, I was already working the Big 10 and the MAC, so my name was getting out there quite a bit in the referee fraternity. What better way to give back to the game than to have a camp to share what I have learned and what I know? There really weren't any significant camps for adult referees going on at the time, so I gave it a shot. That year, the Phil Bova Referee Camp was born.

One of the print ads for the Bova Camp

What would be the best way to help aspiring officials? How could I structure it to give the best bang for the buck to those that really wanted to learn? HOW COULD I BEST HELP PEOPLE IMPROVE THEMSELVES? That was important to me. I have always tried to please people—as that was in my nature— but I had to learn early that was nearly impossible in the officiating business. Still, how could I best help guys (and girls) on their path to becoming better officials?

First and foremost, I wanted my camp attendees to get the most for their time and money. I didn't want to set this up as a lecture series where someone would come and take notes for a couple hours and call it a day. No way. I set it up for a week. It was a full week—living and breathing basketball from the referee's perspective. Equally important was building the brotherhood and camaraderie amongst fellow officials.

The venue was important too. What would make the most sense? To me, it was a natural to partner up with a small local college. Not only would there be plenty of meeting space, but there was also plenty of gym space. I could also then partner with the basketball staff at the school for 'give and take' open conversation. The staff could ask the officials anything they wanted, while the officials could do the same to them. Seemed like a natural...when was there ever an opportunity to have that kind of dialogue? And respectful dialogue on top of it!

Lastly, I would pick a week when there were games going on at the schools. AAU, youth camps, local tournaments, intramurals, you name it. Camp attendees could learn and ask questions in a classroom setting, but then put their skills to use on the floor. That sounds like the best of both worlds, right? I would have camp assistants video tape the games and critique the officials to give honest feedback on their performance.

I thought it was a solid week for aspiring officials. They received real experience, plenty of interaction, and in an intimate setting. I also mixed in guest speakers on occasion to spice things up a bit. Campers would not only leave the week as much better officials, but they also gained a bunch of brothers and sisters in the fraternity of officiating.

In terms of guest speakers, I would sometimes pull local coaches from other schools or even some players from the surrounding area. As grateful as I was for anyone to take time out of their busy schedules, there were two coaches that came that really stood out and had an impact on the group.

The first I'd like to mention is the great Al McGuire. As some of you know, Coach McGuire was the head coach at Marquette from 1964-1977. He also has the distinction of being the first coach ejected from a National Championship game in 1974. Coach Al then won the title in 1977 with Butch Lee and retired from coaching after the game. Talk about going out on top!

Shortly after retiring, McGuire worked for NBC Sports

doing some play-by-play work, and he hosted a show on Saturdays. Well, he and I worked with each other a bit on the floor, and he knew of me and the camp. He found it interesting enough to come speak in front of the group and also do a feature on us for his show. He interacted with the attendees and interviewed a few folks, not to mention yours truly. He couldn't have been more giving of his time and more courteous to those trying to work on their craft.

Legendary coach Al McGuire learning about the Bova Camp

That really meant a lot to me. Coach Al was one of the premier coaches of the generation and a star on NBC. He thought enough of what we were trying to do to spend some time with us to share his thoughts about the game and the coach/referee relationship.

McGuire lost his battle with leukemia in January of 2001. As soon as I heard of his passing, I boarded the first plane I could (commercial, this time!) to Milwaukee to pay my respects to a great coach and a great guy. The Good Lord must have needed someone special to man the clipboard for His team. I arrived in Milwaukee, attended the service, and then headed back to the airport to fly back that evening. He meant that much to me.

A few years later, Bobby Knight came to the camp as a guest speaker. Yes, it was after the 1985 incident that we will discuss later. I'm not sure if he came out of respect to me or as a payback/apology for the chair, but either way, we were glad to have him. Coach Knight was a coaching legend and icon at the time. For him to come to Baldwin Wallace College for our camp was more than flattering. On top of him showing up, he refused to take payment for his appearance or to get reimbursed for his expenses.

The day he arrived, I asked him to stand in the hallway while the attendees and I were chatting in the classroom. During a break in the discussion, I asked the group:

"How many of you would think I'm nuts if I told you Bobby Knight was standing behind that door AND willing to answer any questions you have??"

I'm pretty sure everyone raised their hands. I think some people raised both hands. If they somehow grew a 3rd hand, I'm sure that would have gone up in the air as well.

"Let's put our hands together for Coach Bob Knight!"

In struts Coach Knight. You could see the surprise and the amazement in the eyes of the campers. They almost fell off their chairs. He was such a presence... Not only was he probably the most well-known coach in America, he also had one of the most fiery tempers of anyone to stroll the sidelines. Mix in the fact that Coach stands 6 foot 5 inches, and he was in a small room with everyone, I think the group would have been less intimidated if King Kong walked into the room.

After this legend walked into the room, he took his place at the front podium. I stood off to the side a bit to let him have his monologue and then take control of the question and answer session. He was about to get into it, but looked at me first and said:

"Phil, if you want to sit, I'll throw you a chair…"

Now this guy is a comedian too.

In reality, it was perfection. He lightened the mood a bit from the outset and helped the campers feel at ease. I was hoping to have Coach stick around for an hour or so. Nope. He stood up there and talked to us for THREE HOURS. He answered every question and stayed until there were no questions left.

Coach Knight and I going through some instruction

Near the end of his participation came one of the funniest moments I had ever experienced in all my years of the camp.

This particular year, I had one attendee who was hearing impaired. For the classroom session, this gentleman had an assistant who would use sign language to communicate what was being said. It worked out perfectly...well...until Coach Knight brought his 'R' rated discussion to the table.

How was this poor woman going to communicate all the "mf-er", "a-hole", and "c-sucker" references? At first her hands went a million miles an hour in trying to 'spell' with her hand gestures what Coach was saying. Then it got to be too much, as Coach was just describing things in his own colorful way.

Eventually, it got to the point where the assistant would just

67

wave a hand gesture with every expletive. For example, to relay the "f word", she would make an "ok" symbol with her left hand, and then use the right index finger to jab in and out of the circle she made with her left hand. To describe the oral sex term that Knight would call someone, she opened her mouth and jabbed that same right index finger in and out of her mouth at 100 miles per hour. The dynamic of watching her sign normal conversation with a hand to the mouth every two seconds was a hysterical subplot to Coach's monologue. It would not have surprised me in the least if that young lady had two dozen dinner invitations later that evening.

Coach Knight started to notice the smirks and chuckles as he was speaking and eventually asked the group what was so funny. To her credit, the assistant raised her hand to ask a question. We couldn't wait to see what she had to say. Eventually, she was called on…

"My friend would like to know if you would have any issue with a hearing impaired referee working your game."

Coach Knight thought for a minute and delivered this beauty:

"To be honest with you, 99% of you sons of bitches are blind anyway, so what the hell difference does it make if you can't hear either?"

The room howled with laughter. Classic Bobby Knight.

Either way, this wasn't a publicity stunt, or him looking to get credit for something. This was Coach Knight taking time out of his ridiculous schedule to do something for the betterment of the game. It was incidents like this that he never got the deserved credit for, but showed that even King Kong has a soft side too.

68

Coach Knight accepting a plaque for his participation

I'm proud to say that the camp ran for 23 consecutive years, starting in 1980 and concluding in 2002. Sure, we had a fair share of excellent referees come through that camp…people like Ted Valentine, and a host of others. I tried to keep track of as many graduates as I could over the years, and I was certainly there to help write recommendations on their behalf and at the very least, help in their progression as they tried to work their way through the ranks. I'm sure I missed a few along the way, but at one point I counted 77 camp graduates that had worked their way into college ball from Division 3 to Division 1. Three graduates, Terry Wymer, Mike Roberts, and Ted Valentine have officiated in the Final Four. My staff and I are extremely proud to say that we were an integral part of their success.

I am very pleased that our staff had that much of an impact in the progression of these camp attendees. We were fortunate enough to earn the #1 Camp Ranking from The Book For Referees, and for the amount of time, energy, and preparation we put into it, we definitely earned it!

Our group photo from the 1983 camp at Oberlin College

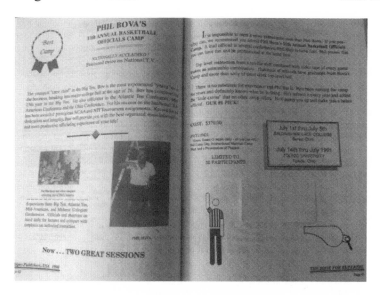

**Extremely honored to be named "Best Camp" and "Our #1 Pick"
by <u>The Book For Referees</u>**

The formula for the camp was fairly simple as I mentioned earlier. It was a full week of intense concentration in improving the ability to officiate the game. At week's end, the group was exhausted after officiating several games, reviewing tapes, and discussions with supervisors. Needless to say, there were some evening activities as well that may or may not have included some adult beverages.

As everyone dragged their weary carcasses to the final group meeting, we ended every week the same way. I took the microphone, put on my PA announcer voice, and introduced each attendee in front of the group for the final time. I asked each of them to say a few words about what the camp meant to them. The learning. The brotherhood. The family atmosphere.

I am pretty sure that every year that we had the camp, there was someone in the corner chopping the strongest onions in

America. Why is that? Simple—for all the individuals we had, there was never a dry eye in the house. Yours truly included. It was an emotional end to a fabulous week of work. It concluded with all of us holding a glass of wine (hey I'm Italian), and toasting to each other. The grand finale was always led by my dear friend Joe Pangrazio. (Joe was the Big 10 observer at Ohio State for 18 years). Joe always had a special prayer prepared and led the entire camp with his words of wisdom.

Joe Pangrazio leading the way

Over the years, so many officiating icons visited our camps. Names like Herm Rohrig, John Payak, Jim Desmond, Bob Wortman, Jim Lessig, George Solomon, Gary Muncy, John Adams, and the great Earl Strom. While I have great memories of so many people, one individual still stands out to this day. Her name is Pat Hardesty.

Pat called me a month before one of the camps started. We exchanged pleasantries for a few moments, and then she told me she would like to attend the camp...but there was a problem. We didn't have TOO many females attending the camp in the years prior, so I wasn't sure what the problem could be. Maybe she was pregnant? Intimidated by being one of the few females with a large group of guys? I wasn't sure what it could be, so I asked Donna to hop on the phone at the same time in case I needed some help from the female perspective.

"Mr. Bova, I would like to attend your camp. I love basketball, but I am not able to play as much anymore. I have Multiple Sclerosis. Can I still come to your camp?"

I didn't know a whole lot about MS, but I knew it was a debilitating disease that caused a lot of pain around the muscles, nerves and joints. It was tough enough to be an official under ideal circumstances; I knew that doing it with this hurdle would take someone special.

"Pat, we would be honored to have you, and we will make it the best week of your life."

Pat Hardesty did come to the camp that year. She worked like crazy, fighting through the adversity that she was given, and she had an unbelievable impact on all of us. Coincidentally, Pat came the same year that Al McGuire made his visit. As expected, Al did the special about the camp and did a feature story on Pat Hardesty. It was wonderful. He featured Pat on his nationally televised college basketball program, and it was a great tribute to a wonderful young lady.

As we did our traditional close to the camp that year, I called all the aspiring officials one by one. The last one was Pat.

"Laaaaddiiiies and Gentlemen.....PAT HARDESTY"

You would have thought the Pope walked through the door. Everyone in attendance—campers and staff—were up on their feet giving her a standing ovation that would have rivaled any ovation I have ever seen before. I think we had a dozen onion choppers in the room that day, as the tears were flowing. If someone wasn't crying at that point, I would have approached them to make sure they still had a pulse.

It was truly one of the most beautiful moments that I have ever shared with a group in a basketball setting. In life, you just never know when your emotions will be brought to tears. It's what you take from the moments that make you a better person on and off the floor. Pat Hardesty's commitment and dedication made an impression that would last a lifetime.

Pat Hardesty was an inspiration to us all

"I asked a ref if he could give me a technical foul for thinking bad things about him. He said, of course not. I said, well, I think you stink. And he gave me a technical. You can't trust 'em"

-Jim Valvano

6

Flirting with the NBA

Naturally, it's the dream of any high school basketball player to play college basketball. A step further, it's a similar dream of college players to make it to the NBA. I guess the same could be said of other occupations…most people want to make it to the top level, to the ultimate.

I've often been asked if I have ever wanted to leave the college game and officiate in the NBA. The life of an NBA referee is significantly different than their counterparts in the NCAA. That said, I did toy with the idea in the mid-70s. Here's what happened:

In the 1970s, I was on a fast path up the charts in the officiating community. I was doing MAC games in 1975 and the Big 10 in 1976, and I thought the next natural step was the NBA. Prior to the 1977 season, I was selected to 'audition' at an NBA referee's camp in New Orleans. Nick Mileti, who was the Cleveland Cavaliers owner at the time, wrote a letter on my behalf to suggest my inclusion to the camp. Ray Dieringer also spoke up on my behalf, which again, was a great thrill.

Dear Mr. Nucatola:

I would like to take this opportunity to recommend a young man who, I feel, will certainly be a PLUS as an official and a gentleman to the professional ranks.

I have observed Mr. Bova for the last three years and needless to say, since then he stepped forward and worked to get a schedule, and I have never seen an official develop so quickly.

He has completely dedicated himself to officiating and I am sure you will see this in his performances both on the floor and off.

He also has a professional background in baseball so these pressures aren't going to shake this man in close situations.

He has command, respect, temperament with the desire to execute his job properly, and is willing to learn; so I feel he has what you are looking fo

May I, Mr. Ray Dieringer, head basketball coach at Cleveland State Universi recommend highly to you without reservation, a capable man.

If further information is needed, please feel free to call on me.

Sincerely,

Ray Dieringer

Eternally grateful to Ray for speaking up on my behalf

I did well at the camp. So well, that I was chosen to attend a second camp in California to further sharpen my skills for the pro game. The California camp was intended to be for those that were the cream of the crop in New Orleans. Once California concluded, the NBA would choose which officials to bring on and be part of the rotation.

Plenty of good seats still available...

In 1976-77, the NBA only had 22 teams, but they still played an 82 game schedule. John Nucatola was the NBA Supervisor of Officials for the NBA, and he had a staff of 26 regular officials. These referees would fly all over the country to officiate games for the regular season and playoffs. It was a lot of

work for a relatively small pool of officials, so they were looking
to increase the staff to ease the burden.

In April of the 1976-77 season, the NBA officials went on
strike after the regular season ended, but before the playoffs
started. The contract that the referees were working under ended
the last day of the regular season.   The officials at the time did not
want to work in good faith until another contract was ratified. Out
of the 26 officials, 24 were part of the Union and carried out the
walkout. Richie Powers and Earl Strom were not part of the Union
and continued to work.

The NBA had to scramble. Playoffs were about to begin,
and they did not have officials to work the games. They began to
reach down to the training camps and offered positions to those
that had earned the highest marks in the training sessions.
Substitute officials were being offered $300 per game, $40 per
diem, and first class airfare for each game they were assigned.
That was less than the $335 average per game rate that the striking
officials were getting, but a pretty good buck nonetheless.

Guess who got the call.

I had a choice to make. I could get my foot in the door in
the NBA and begin doing games in their time of need. Surely, I
would be rewarded long term for helping them out of a jam, right?
This could lead to a long-term career in the pros jet setting all over
the country and making a good salary. Plus, I would be reffing
games with guys like Pistol Pete Maravich, George Gervin, and
Dr. J? Are you kidding me??

That all sounded well and good, but I had to look at the
other side too. How would it affect my home life?   I would go
from working games in Columbus and East Lansing, to places like
Phoenix, San Antonio, and Los Angeles. I would never be home.

Could I cross the picket line? Could I step over what my fellow officials were fighting for and stab them in the back? More importantly—my father was in the Cleveland Police Union….could I jump a picket line and disappoint him by not supporting the cause for what my brothers were fighting for?

Hell no.

I called Nucatola back and respectfully declined to cross the picket line. If he chose to call me back when the strike was settled and offer me a position, I told him that I would consider the opportunity.

The strike lasted a short while. The NBA had the integrity of the playoffs to consider, not to mention the negative feedback by the fans. On top of that, the replacement referees were constantly in harm's way from fans and regular officials alike. It was getting to be an ugly situation that the NBA had to solve quickly. And they did.

The 1976-77 season ended with the Portland Trailblazers taking out the Philadelphia 76ers in 6 games. Bill Walton took home the NBA Finals MVP honors.

I didn't think I would hear from John Nuctola again, since I had turned down the offer to work the NBA during the previous season. I was already thinking ahead to my Big 10 and MAC schedules for the upcoming fall and winter.

Wrong.

Nucatola called and asked if I would consider joining his crew of officials for the 1977-78 season. Instead of the full 82 game schedule, I was offered 41 games as a part-time official.

I had to go through the same thought process as I did the

79

first time he called. The 41 game schedule would not have me away from home as much as 82, but still a good amount. I would also have to give up my position as an educator. There was no way I could travel to some of these games and still be home to make it to school the next morning. The NBA would run me ragged all over the country, while I still had some ability to control my college schedule. The NBA was more money, but I wasn't convinced it was more happiness. The kids at school needed me. My family needed me.

"Thank you, Mr. Nucatola, but again, I will have to pass on your offer."

It sounds kind of crazy when I think to myself that "I turned down the NBA", but I have no regrets. Do I wonder what it would have been like jetting all over the country and working with the best players in the world? Sure. I wouldn't have it any other way though. I was in my own bed most nights and had the pleasure to work at some of the finest institutions in the country.

I kept my morals, my family, and my teaching position while making my dad proud.

I did the right thing.

Don't you think it's strange how many referees work at Foot Locker?

-Jim Gaffigan

7

Selection Sunday

Just like our friends that are playing the game at these institutions, the NCAA Tournament is the pinnacle for Division 1 basketball officials. To get selected to participate in these games is not only a difficult process, but also a rewarding experience.

The vast majority of officials across the country belong to conferences, or at least have a primary conference that they claim allegiance. Since conferences don't play every single game of the week, many guys will work for other conferences as well to increase the amount of games they can do in a season. As mentioned earlier, I did the Big 10…and I also worked for the MAC, Atlantic 10, and did some Horizon games on occasion. I would work an average of 50 contests per year. Some guys did way less, some did more—it really just depended on each guy's personal situation.

After working the non-conference schedule, and then the regular season, most conferences had a post season tournament to determine the champion of the league and who would earn the automatic berth to the NCAA Tournament.

For each of these leagues, it was their time to shine. The bigger conferences host their season ending tournament in big arenas at neutral sites, while some of the smaller conferences play at member schools. In nearly all cases, the finals (and most of the rounds preceding it) were broadcast on national television. It's the perfect appetizer for the NCAA Tournament that would take place the following week.

As we all head toward "Selection Sunday," the power conferences have a pretty good idea who is going to get in, while the really little guys know their conference will only send one team. The mid-major schools would be somewhere in the middle, sending somewhere between two and five teams to the Big Dance.

From the referee side of things, it's a pretty similar situation. The Supervisor of Officials from each conference would compile data on these referees, from attending game supervisors and from conference coaches as well. From these resources, the Supervisor would submit the ranking/list to the National Supervisor of Officials. Certainly, guys that were highest on the list had the best chance to be selected to the NCAA Tournament games. If you were ranked high on lists from MULTIPLE conferences (like I was fortunate enough to be), your chances to be picked were even greater.

In a similar way to the teams, big conferences sent more of their officials to the Tournament than did the smaller ones. The Big 10, ACC, Big 12 etc, were going to have more representation than would conferences like the Ivy, Big West, etc. Fair or not, that's just the way it was.

Once the National Supervisor of Officials and his selection committee have the recommendation lists from all conferences, they then determine how many from each conference will make the cut. Not counting the First Four games that have been part of the tournament since 2011, 96 officials get selected to work the first round of the Dance. 32 first round games, three officials per game, and voila, 96 whistle blowers.

Just like our friends that are actually playing the game, referees wait by the phone on Selection Sunday too. Once the teams get selected to their locations for the first round games, the National Coordinator will finish off the task of assigning 12 officials to each of the eight locations for the First Round. Those that follow the Tournament closely know that each First Round location hosts four games on that opening Thursday or Friday. There are two doubleheaders at each site on that venue's opening day.

So, on that Sunday night, those participating in the Tournament will get the call and the venue that you have been assigned to. It goes a little something like this:

"Congratulations, Mr. Bova, you have been assigned to the First Round of the NCAA Tournament's West Region. Your game is Thursday in Dallas, Texas. Please arrive to the site city the day before the game."

There you go. Now you have to come up with a plan on how to get to Dallas by Wednesday. I know I have mentioned it more than a couple times, but this is where your support system comes into play. TGFD. Not only do I have to get all arrangements made to get to, and stay in, a city I have never been to, but need to do it quickly. Naturally, everything at home still goes on as normal, and Donna would take up the slack to make sure the kids (and everything else) doesn't skip a beat.

You may have noticed that in the sample message above, I did not say which GAME of the four to be played I would be doing. That comes later.

Come Monday, the actual times of the games get announced, AND which games will be played at those specific times. For hypothetical sake, let's assume that Dallas has Noon, 2:30, 6:00, and 8:30 start times. I'm not sure how they decide which games get assigned to which time slot, but they aren't going to let a referee do a game that he has an allegiance to. If I was originally told that I would be getting the 2:30 game...and then Ohio State gets assigned the 2:30 time slot...well, that wouldn't make a whole lot of sense. It IS possible for an official who works multiple conferences to get a team he has had before, but naturally they try to avoid that.

By Wednesday (or Thursday if your venue starts on Friday), each of the officials arrive in town. More often than not, they were guys that you didn't know or have any sort of history with, as these guys were arriving from different conferences and from all parts of the country. Of course, if you had some buddies that were moving on to the Tournament, you could always check and see where they ended up and IF they ended up in the same city you did.

The next day, Thursday morning, the tournament city hosts a breakfast for the dozen officials that were selected to officiate the games that day. During that breakfast, you were told which game you would be doing that day. The 12 officials were also informed who would be doing the second round too. It was very unlikely that the six officials ONLY working one game had a chance to advance to the Regional games.

So, if you had the nooner, you would be heading to work soon. If you had the 8:30pm contest, you had a whole bunch of time to kill before you threw the striped shirt on. You could stick around and watch some games, hang out in the hotel all day, whatever you wanted. No matter what you decided, you had to be

SURE you were in the arena at least two hours before tip time.

During my run of 20 straight Tournaments, I had the pleasure of working all of those time slots. I really preferred doing the early game. You could get your work in and have the balance of the day to do as you pleased. On the flip side, the late game was by far my least favorite time. When you head to that breakfast in the morning, the adrenaline is flowing and the butterflies are flapping their wings already…and to have to temper that and simmer down for 10-12 hours until you work, wasn't that appealing. Speaking of not appealing, I also didn't prefer to work the 1-16, or 2-15 matchup. Really, I wasn't a fan of doing any game that was anticipated as being a blowout. Here's why…

Cities that hosted First Round games also hosted Second Round games just 2 days later. In the Dallas example, the four Thursday games would produce four winners and four losers, with the winners obviously advancing to the second round on Saturday. On the referee side, of the 12 guys already in the city, only six are needed to work those two Saturday games.

In tight games, you can really show what you can do. How do you handle the situation, the ultra-sensitive and tense coaches, the bright lights, and the big time? By working blow outs, both teams are coasting to the end with the outcome already determined. You are giving 100% and your best either way, but the situations to attempt to further prove yourself are clearly different. If Kansas is beating North Valley Tech State by 45 with 10 minutes to play, there is only so much you can do!

Once the first week is complete, everyone heads home. The 16 teams still alive know where they are headed next, as all they need to do is look at the bracket. The guys in stripes head home and wait for the call for next week's action. The original group of 96 guys gets knocked down to 36 for the Sweet 16 and Elite 8 round.

The next week follows the Thursday through Sunday format, with only four sites this time. Each site will host four teams on Thursday or Friday, with the two winners advancing to Saturday or Sunday, respectively. For this week's games, 10 officials are selected for each site. Three guys each will work Sweet 16 Game #1, Sweet 16 Game #2, and the Elite 8 game in each host city. The 10th official works as a "stand by" for all three games in case one of the officials can't continue working the game due to injury or illness. If you are fortunate enough to receive a call for this round of games, you are told the host city and the day you are working so that your travel can be planned accordingly. The obvious difference from this round versus the last is that there is no opportunity to work multiple games on that weekend.

Once those games are complete, that leaves us the Final Four. These games are usually played in massive venues that can hold large amounts of people. They aren't traditional basketball arenas, but ever since Magic/Bird in 1979, the popularity of the Tournament has exploded.

In similar fashion, the officials and teams head home following the Elite 8 round. Again, the schools know where they are headed next, as Final Four destinations are determined a few years in advance. The pool of 36 guys that were working on the Sweet 16 weekend gets chopped down again to a lucky 10 guys. Of those 10, three guys will work each semi-final, and three guys will work the championship game. There is an additional official selected to be on hand as an alternate in case something negative happens to one of the guys working the game. The NCAA absolutely does not want only two guys working a game—no matter the reason—on its biggest stage.

The guys chosen to work the Final Four games on Saturday need to be in town by Friday. The lucky three that will work the Final on Monday are asked not to arrive in town until Sunday. I'm guessing the NCAA wants to keep the identities of those officials under wraps as long as possible for precautionary reasons.

Bottom line, to be chosen to work the NCAA Tournament is a tremendous honor and thrill. If I think back to my days working CYO ball games and gradually climbing the ladder, the thought of being considered one of the best 96 officials in the country is mind boggling. How many referees are there from the D3 level to the small schools, to mid majors, to majors? Thousands I'm sure. To be recognized as one of the best of the best for two straight decades is something I am very proud of.

Though I was fortunate in doing several games, I have never been really fond of the determining process. I had some friends that were GREAT officials, guys that were doing 75-80 games a year, and never had the opportunity to sniff the games in March. It's still a very subjective process. Year to year, I would have some frustration at times in only doing a game or two in the tournament. As much as I asked the question as to why, I could never get a clear answer. Being a competitive guy, I wanted to know what I could do to better my chances at advancing farther. Instead, I kept my head down and continued to give all I had.

If you look at the history of officials working the Final Four, you tend to see the same names over and over again. Sure, they were guys near the top of the profession, but there are a ton of others near the top that never had the opportunity. Two officials that come to mind are Steve Welmer and Verl Sell.

Steve worked multiple conferences and had several weeks a year where he would be working SIX games a week. Imagine the travel schedule and commitment! Steve often officiated the Conference Championship games in the leagues he worked. While he was selected to work the NCAA Tournament year after year, Steve was never chosen to work the Final Four. That was very puzzling to me and the rest of the officiating community.

Verl Sell primarily worked the Big Ten Conference for well over 20 years. I had the good fortune to work with Verl on many of the top games. Despite working one of the best conferences in the country for over two decades, he was never even selected to work the NCAA Tournament. How is that even possible?

Give officials an opportunity, a reward, for their commitment and dedication year after year. With so many good officials working the game, there is no need for the same guys to be working the Final Four over, and over, and over again. In my opinion, no official should be working back to back Final Fours. There's simply no need.

Truth be told, the NCAA Tournament is such a fabulous event. I have often said that I wished that all Division 1 teams could be included so that the kids at the small schools could enjoy the moment as well. Those kids work every bit as hard as the players at the big schools, but just don't have the same ability as the others. I know it's not feasible and probably not logical to have the Top 25 teams to have to play schools that no one has heard of in the first few rounds, but still I wish that there was a way to make it happen. There just isn't anything like it. The hype, the drama, the pageantry, and the experience are something that every player that participates will never forget. In a perfect world, all college basketball players could enjoy it, even if just for 1 game. I was truly blessed to work the tournament for 20 straight years.

"I hope your seeing eye dog bites you!"

-Wisconsin Fan

8

Top 15 Games

During my career, I have done well over 1,500 games at the collegiate level. I've done everything from Division 3 games in front of 100 people (that number probably includes ticket takers and hot dog vendors) to the Elite 8 in the NCAA Tournament. While there are dozens of memorable games and instances, I thought about trying to narrow it down to a Top 10. That was too hard, so I am going to give you my Top 15 games that I had the good fortune of working.

These choices aren't necessarily games with the most on the line, or buzzer beater finishes, but games that were the most memorable to me. You will find that some have some sort of historical importance, and some that you wouldn't necessarily have read much about in the next day's newspaper.

Here's my Top 15.

#15) *5 Overtime Game-Wow*

Central Michigan at Toledo

Toledo, OH

March 4, 1978

I was only a couple years in to the officiating thing when this game was put on my schedule. From all accounts, it should have been a snoozer since the Chips were sitting at 11-10, and Toledo was closing out the home schedule with a fine record of 18-5. The previously mentioned Bob Wortman was my partner that day.

Toledo had just beaten Miami a couple days prior and were tied with the Redskins (yes, Miami was the Redskins then!) with a single game to play. Going into that Saturday, Toledo needed to beat Central, while Miami had to win at Ball State to share the conference crown. Toledo and Miami split the season series—so I'm not sure how they would have decided the automatic bid to the NCAA tournament, but that ticket to the Big Dance was on the line.

Miami handled their business that day in a 74-67 win at Ball State. Toledo needed the victory over the Chippewas to keep pace. My partner and I knew the stakes on the line for that game, and we were ready to go from the tip. I say partner—singular—because the NCAA had not moved to 3-man crews yet.

The game was pretty typical, the normal see-saw affair. Central was playing loose with nothing to lose, while the Rockets were clearly wound a little tightly with a share of the conference title line. Moving ahead to the end of regulation, the buzzer went off with the teams knotted up at 62. We are going to overtime.

The teams went back and forth during that overtime and ended that extra frame still deadlocked. This time, we were tied at 68. We headed to a second extra session.

The teams went back and forth during that overtime and ended that extra frame still deadlocked. This time, we were tied at 76. We headed to a third extra session.

The teams went back and forth during that overtime and ended that extra frame still deadlocked. This time, we were tied at 88. We headed to a fourth extra session.

The teams went back and forth during that overtime......you know where I am going with this, right?? Yep, you got it, overtime #4 ended in a 97-97 tie.

By this time, my partner and I were absolutely gassed. Luckily this game happened earlier in my career when I was still in good shape and kept up with these gazelles running up and down the floor. With the four overtimes, we had already worked an entire extra half of basketball. And with only two guys in stripes patrolling the floor, we exerted ourselves about as much as any official in the history of basketball. Funny thing—we weren't done yet.

On to overtime #5. This time Central went ahead for good on a put back by Jeff Tropf, taking a 104-103 lead. After a couple traded baskets, Central went ahead 109-105 on a couple free throws with five seconds left. Toledo added a garbage time basket to cut the deficit to two, but too little too late. Central Michigan 109, Toledo 107 in 5 OT. Adios to a share of the MAC title for Toledo, and no NCAA Tournament for the Rocket supporters. It was a devastating loss for Toledo.

I'm not sure if it was the last 5 OT game for a 2-man crew, but if not, it had to have been one of the last, as those kinds of games don't happen often. I drank so much liquid that day, I'm pretty sure my molars were treading water on my drive home.

#14) *The Legend of Shaquille O'Neal*

Villanova vs LSU

Springfield, MA

November 24, 1990

I felt very blessed to be selected to work this game. After all, neither one of these teams were in a conference that I was affiliated with. This game was part of the Hall of Fame Tipoff Classic, with proceeds naturally benefitting the Basketball Hall of Fame in Springfield. While this wasn't the 'official' opening of college basketball's season, it was a high profile, national TV game.

Just eight months earlier, the Wildcats and Tigers met in Tennessee in the First Round of the NCAA Tournament. With Mahmoud Abdul Rauf, and the twin towers of Stanley Roberts and Shaquille O'Neal leading the way, the Tigers posted a 70-63 win.

The start of the 1990 season featured the rematch. With Abdul-Raul and Roberts gone, how would super-soph Shaquille O'Neal do on his own? Could Coach Rollie Massimino come up with a plan to handle the big fella and get revenge?

I was excited to see this guy play. With O'Neal in a different part of the country and not crossing paths with my conferences, this was likely the only time I would have him. The national media painted this guy as a freak of nature—so big, strong, agile, and nearly unstoppable.

They were right. This guy was unbelievable. I've often said that Big Dog Robinson at Purdue was the best I had seen consistently in college, but this one time shot of O'Neal….he was a different animal. I'm a referee—not a scout—but this guy had 'no doubt about it' written all over him in regard to being the next big thing at the pro level.

Coach Mass and I exchanged some Italian greetings before the game, and I had Coach Dale Brown for the first time. Very nice guy. And we were all here to put some funds in the pocket of the Hall of Fame.

The game itself was almost inconsequential. Greg Woodard from Villanova stole the show by knocking down six of eight 3-pointers and finishing with 28 points. Shaq was in foul trouble much of the 2nd half but had the chance to put the Tigers up in the late going. Down 92-91, O'Neal missed a baseline jumper that could have put LSU up. Instead, Lance Miller from the Wildcats came up with a rebound and was fouled with three seconds left. He knocked down one of two free throws for the game's final margin. Villanova 93, LSU 91.

O'Neal went on to average 28 points and 15 rebounds that sophomore season. Of course, we all know what happened from there.

#13) *MAC Championship in my Hometown*

Ball State vs Miami (OH)

Cleveland, OH

March 8, 2000

For the 10 years prior to the 2000 event, the MAC Tournament rotated amongst host cities, Toledo, Detroit and Columbus. Starting in 2000, the MAC made Gund/Quicken Loans Arena in Cleveland its permanent home.

The championship game of this tournament was one I wanted badly. I had already been a regular official in the conference for more than two decades, and this was the FIRST one in my hometown. For me, that gave it a little extra juice. Not only could I make it to the arena in 20 minutes, but I could also invite my friends and family to the game without the inconvenience of extra travel.

Fortunately, I got the call.

I was very proud to take the floor that day. I know it was all about the teams that made it to the title game, and it was about the kids that worked to get there. On the inside I got that same type of feeling you get when you return to the old neighborhood or to your high school when you have accomplished something to be proud of. It was a great feeling. I felt like I was hosting the game!

Ball State was the #2 seed coming in, having a first round bye and won two games to reach the final. Miami was the #9 seed and made an improbable run. The boys from Oxford won three games (including beating the #1 seed Bowling Green) to reach the Final. The Red Hawks reached the final game with a 15-14 record—one win from a MAC Tournament title and berth in the Big Dance. On the other side, the Ball State Cardinals that were led by Duane Clemens brought a 20-8 mark to the game.

It was a great game. There were 11 lead changes in the first half alone, before the Red Hawks took a 34-33 lead into the

94

half. After the break, the Cards used an 11-2 run to jump ahead by eight. Miami fought back and took a 52-51 lead with under five minutes to play. From that point on, it was all Cardinals as they eventually pulled away. The final was Ball State 61, Miami 56.

For their efforts, Ball State drew UCLA in the first round, and they lasted for only that game. As any mid-major will tell you, the goal is to win the conference. When you get to the NCAA Tournament, you are really playing with house money. The 2000 MAC Tournament in Cleveland was definitely house money for me.

#12) *Elite 8 Game in Los Angeles*

Arizona vs Missouri

Los Angeles, CA

March 26, 1994

I am very proud to say that I was selected for the NCAA Tournament for TWENTY straight years. It's difficult enough to be selected to the tournament at all, as you need to be among the best in your conference to even be considered. And even if selected, the majority of guys only work one game before their season ends.

After a couple early round games, I was chosen to do this particular game in the NCAA Tournament. This was the Elite Eight game in the West region being played at the Los Angeles Sports Arena, in the shadow of the LA Coliseum and just south of the USC campus. At the time, the Sports Arena was home to the

LA Clippers.

This was my first Elite Eight, which is special in its own right. It was even more special that they chose an Ohio guy to fly across the country to do the game. As you can imagine, there are plenty of good officials on that side of the Mississippi, and to have my number called to do a game of such importance was truly special. Needless to say, the winner was headed to the Final Four, and that's as big as it gets for programs and coaches in college hoops.

Truthfully, I had some butterflies approaching the game. These were two teams I have never had, in a state I never worked…let alone the arena and the stakes were never higher. Missouri came in at 27-3, while Arizona was 28-5. I had never worked with the great Norm Stewart before, but I did have Lute in Iowa a number of times before he headed to Tucson.

The atmosphere was very clearly different. This was my first real taste on the big stakes of college basketball. Every possession mattered. The crowd and players were living and dying with each shot. The intensity was incredible. This was truly the big time.

Unfortunately, the game itself didn't live up to its billing. After the Wildcats took a 48-34 lead at the break, Arizona cruised to a 92-72 win. Khalid Reeves and Damon Stoudamire combined for 55 points, while Big 8 Player of the Year, Melvin Booker, had 14. Missouri shot 35% from the floor and were never a threat.

The 'cats went to the Final Four and lost the semifinal to Nolan Richardson's Arkansas Razorbacks. Richardson's "40 Minutes of Hell" wore down Arizona, and then the Hogs eventually beat Duke to win the National Title.

While I was hopeful to follow the Wildcats to Charlotte for the Final Four, it wasn't meant to be. I was able to witness the enormity of college basketball on a national level. Of course, I had done league championship games, big rivalries, and Top 10 matchups before, but this was just a whole different ball of wax. The 1979 Final between Magic and Larry Bird really put the NCAA Tournament on the map, and it's gotten bigger and better ever since.

#11) *The Mob vs The Mormons*

UNLV vs Utah

Seattle, WA

March 21, 1991

The 1991 Tournament afforded me the first opportunity to do a Sweet 16 matchup, and what an assignment it was. I got the defending champion UNLV Runnin' Rebels who were 32-0 entering the game and hoping to be the first team since Bob Knight's Hoosiers to finish a season unbeaten. The Utes on the other side just survived a 2 OT thriller against Michigan State and were 27-3.

On the sidelines was the great Rick Majerus for Utah, God rest his soul… One of the great guys in the profession and he was certainly one of the most entertaining. On the other side, we had the legendary "Tark the Shark", Jerry Tarkanian. Fairly or unfairly, Tark was under the watchful eye of the NCAA for nearly his whole career. Needless to say, eyebrows were raised when he put together a MONSTER of a program at a school in the desert that was mostly a commuter school. I mean, it was Vegas right? Everything HAD to have been on the up and up, right?!

The interesting thing about this game was that it was in Seattle. Again, I was as honored as could be that they chose me to fly across the country to officiate the game. But—this time, the game was in a dome, not a regular sized basketball arena. The Seattle Kingdome was home to the Mariners and Seahawks, and it would now host the Sweet 16 matchup. It was certainly a different perspective for all involved to be in such a cavernous environment. Like anything else, once there, everyone adjusted accordingly. When I saw a "Mormons vs the Mob" sign, I got a good laugh and was ready to go.

Anyway, UNLV had won 44 straight dating back to the previous season, and they started off slowly with a 41-35 lead. Coach Tark was sucking on his towel like he famously did. I'm told that the towel was soaked with water to keep his whistle wet. To this day, I'm not convinced it wasn't soaked in vodka.

In the second half, the Rebels pulled away behind Larry Johnson and Stacey Augmon, cruising to an 83-66 win. The Rebels were athletic and played fast…probably the best college team I had seen play over my 30 years. Tark and Company made the Final Four again that season, and shockingly lost the semi-final matchup against Duke, ending their season at 34-1. I was surprised. Those guys were good. Real good. It was fun to be on the floor with them.

10) *Coaching Drama*

Iowa vs Illinois

Champaign, IL

February 4, 1993

Illinois vs Iowa sounds like a typical Big 10 fistfight, right? No…this one is a little different. It had a little extra juice to it and the atmosphere was fantastic.

A few years earlier in 1989, Bruce Pearl was an assistant at Iowa. At the time, Deon Thomas was a prized Chicago recruit who was trying to decide between Illinois and Iowa to play his college ball. Pearl felt that the Hawkeyes were losing the battle for Thomas and took matters into his own hands.

During a phone conversation with Thomas, Pearl flipped on a tape recorder and legally recorded a conversation. In Iowa, it was legal to do that, but not in Illinois. Either way, Thomas didn't know he was being recorded. During the conversation, Pearl accused an Illinois assistant of offering Thomas $80,000 and a Chevy Blazer to choose Illinois. Pearl's set of leading questions got Thomas to "admit" that the offer had been made. Of course, that was illegal recruiting.

The recorded conversation led to an NCAA investigation. Thomas said that he agreed to whatever Pearl said to get him off the phone as quickly as possible. The ensuing investigation led to Thomas to have to sit during his first year of eligibility, and Illinois being hit with harsh sanctions for failure to control the basketball program. All said, the NCAA could not prove further wrong doing, but the Illini were still hit with penalties, and Thomas had to sit an entire year.

For the next several years, any time Iowa came to town, the Illini faithful were ruthless. To say they were angry at all-things Iowa is an understatement. Even though Pearl left to take the Southern Indiana job, the Hawkeyes still paid the price.

Illinois was 12-6 at the time, while the Hawkeyes were having an outstanding year. Led by Acie Earl, Iowa came into the game at 12-3 and #9 in the country. They had just beaten the Fab Five in Iowa City and were riding high.

The game was about as intense as any I can remember— especially for a regular season game. It's hard to describe what it was like…one of those times that you really had to BE there to really get the full appreciation.

The game was a back-and-forth affair like most Big 10 games are. To keep a long story short, Iowa 'won' 77-75 on a Jim Bartels basket as the buzzer sounded. The black and gold celebrated like crazy as they ran through the band and toward the locker room.

Not so fast…

A time out was called, and the buzzer had sounded too quickly. Jody Sylvester, Ted Valentine, and I got together and determined that there should be 1.5 seconds back on the clock. We had to get the Hawkeyes back on the floor.

After the chaos had settled, Illinois had to inbound the ball under their own basket with 1.5 seconds to play. Only a miracle play could save the Illini at this point.

Coach Davis put one of his bigs on the inbounder to make it more difficult to make the pass. Since it was a made basket, an

Illinois player screened the defender on the ball and allowed the inbounding player to run the baseline and make a pass without much opposition.

TJ Wheeler made the inbound pass. Everyone in the gym knew it would go to Deon Thomas in the lane or to Andy Kauffman near the half court line. He went with Kauffman who had created some space.

It was a perfect pass. Kauffman caught it in stride between the half court and 3-point lines, took one dribble to get himself into a shooting rhythm, and let it fly.

Swish.

I threw my hands in the air to signify that it was a 3-pointer. Ball game. Illinois 78, Iowa 77.

The. Place. Went. Crazy. Fans rushed the floor. Kauffman got buried in a sea of humanity. The Illini players couldn't believe they had just won in a jarring turn of events. The Hawkeyes—who were celebrating similarly just a few minutes before—were headed to the locker room in a state of disbelief. Complete pandemonium.

I was on the opposite side of the floor from Kauffman's leaning 3-point shot. I started walking toward the scorer's table to be sure they could see me, but quickly thought better of it and headed away from the mob scene before I got swallowed up as well.

Without question, that was probably the most fantastic of finishes that I had seen in my career. The storyline leading up to the game just kicked it up a notch more.

By the way, Deon Thomas—who admitted to being extra amped up for Iowa games ended up with 14 points. The next year, he concluded his career as the leading scorer in Illinois basketball history.

9) *Bruce Pearl and Jimmy Collins*

Wisconsin Milwaukee vs Illinois-Chicago

Chicago, IL

February 7, 2002

The 2001-2002 season saw Wisconsin-Milwaukee move from the Midwestern Collegiate Conference to the Horizon League. That move coincided with Bruce Pearl's first year on the job in Milwaukee after 10 seasons at Southern Indiana. It also guaranteed that the Panthers would be playing Illinois-Chicago twice a year.

As I mentioned above, there was an Illinois assistant that Bruce Pearl had thrown under the bus. That assistant was Jimmy Collins. Collins remained on the Illinois staff and hoped to eventually take the reins of the program. When Lou Henson finally retired in 1996, Illinois bypassed Collins, and instead gave the job to Lon Kruger from Florida. Many felt the Deon Thomas situation cost Collins the chance at the job. Collins then left Illinois after the snub and took the head coaching position at Illinois-Chicago.

Collins was extremely bitter at the entire situation. He felt that his reputation was scarred, that he missed out on the job he really wanted, and that his family was put through unnecessary anguish. The NCAA never did prove anything, and Collins was never charged with any wrong doing. Collins pointed the finger squarely at Pearl for doing this to him.

Five years later, Collins brought his UIC team to Milwaukee to take on Pearl. Leading up to the game, much was made about the two coaches facing each other for the first time. What would happen? How would they react? Well, the game was a blowout, as Wisconsin-Milwaukee blasted the Flames 75-49. The coaches did not shake hands or exchange greetings.

A month later, the Panthers had to make the return to Chicago. Pearl heads to Collins' gym …Collins is already salty from the allegations, and the team is looking for revenge from the beat-down earlier in the season. That's the game I had.

I remember walking into the UIC Pavilion and the tension was so thick, you'd need a chainsaw to cut through it. Collins was still angry, while Pearl was anxious to put the whole episode into the rearview mirror, as this was not a good look for HIM either.

We went through the normal pre-game protocol, but you could tell there was some serious bad blood. Granted, these were basketball super powers doing battle, but there were two basketball junkies at serious odds. The UIC team knew the situation. The Flame fans knew as well. They were ruthless, and Milwaukee was in the lion's den.

The details of the game don't matter much, but UIC pulled out a squeaker, 73-71. In my opinion—and strictly my opinion—if Collins could have fired off a double middle finger salute to Pearl without consequence, he would have.

Later on in the *The News-Gazette*, Collins was quoted as

saying:

"I will never, ever forget what he put me, our staff, my family and the University through. It was so bogus and it was so full of lies. Years ago, I might have been able to hate. But at this point with all the blessings I've received in life, it's virtually impossible for me to hate. But I can tell you this, I don't like him. I never will like him. And I will never pretend by faking the handshakes. Those were really, really troubled times for me."

That's about as tense a game as I had ever done. I am as impartial as they come, but I think the Basketball Karma Gods were smiling on Jimmy and the Flames that night.

#8) *Should have listened to the Supervisor...*

Ohio State vs Wisconsin

Madison, WI

February 2, 1980

Eldon Miller and the Buckeyes had a nice team this season, spending most of it in the Top 10 in the country. They were coming off an embarrassing 20 point home loss to Michigan State, but still sported a 13-4 record heading into the game in Madison. The Badgers were only 10-9 but had already beaten the Buckeyes in Columbus just a week earlier. Logic would dictate the Bucks get their revenge that night.

Just like the old adage goes… "that's why they play the game…" Throw logic out the window. Though the Bucks had a

37-31 lead at the half, Wisconsin came back and beat Ohio State for the second time in about a week; this time by a final score of 70-67. There's no doubt, frustrations boiled over for the Buckeye team and staff after the last couple weeks they had.

After the game, the other officials and I headed to the locker room to clean up and head out. Herm Rohrig, who was the Supervisor of Officials at the time, happened to be at the game and met us in the locker room after to critique our performance.

Just then, there was a knock at the door. One of the Ohio State assistants wanted a piece of us. Clearly, it was OUR fault that they were in a tailspin. Rohrig was fantastic. He told the assistant—Chuck Machok—to shut his mouth, and if he had something to say to report it to the league office. We didn't have time for shenanigans…we had a plane to catch to get out of town. Machok was irritated, just as the rest of the team was.

We got out of there as quickly as we could and arrived to the Madison airport on time. We boarded the plane and prepared for the trip back.

As luck would have it, guess who boarded the plane behind us? Yep, the Ohio State team and Coach Machok. We minded our own business and didn't even make eye contact with this guy. Machok slithered down the aisle, got to our row, and said to my partner loud enough for everyone to hear, "YOU STINK", as well as a few other choice words not fit to print.

We let it go, choosing to take the high road. The plane took off without incident and eventually landed in Milwaukee. Upon arrival, my partners deplaned and needed to catch the next plane headed for Detroit. I deplaned and needed to head to Cleveland. The OSU players, Machok, and Coach Miller got off the plane too and head toward the terminal.

Now the terminal is wide open, and all of us are beginning to figure out the next move. Machok approached me and started to make some disparaging remarks about one of my partners.

Bad idea.

That's it. I've had it. I got right in his face and said:

"Who the hell do you think you're talking to?"

I was dead wrong for doing that. But you know what? I didn't care. I was protecting my guys who called a good game. This is the brotherhood of officials that I keep talking about. I'm certain they would have done the same for me.

Seconds after my attempt at manual voice box removal surgery on Machok, others intervened and separated us. Coach Miller helped restrain Machok, and then the situation was diffused. I'm pretty sure I made my point with him…and didn't have any issues with him ever again.

#7) *The Crown Jewel*

Temple vs Massachusetts

Amherst, MA

March 11, 1993

This game was the Final of the Atlantic 10 Tournament. The first couple rounds were played at the fabulous Palestra in Philadelphia, while the Final was played in Amherst on the home floor of the UMass Minutemen.

This game meant a lot to me. As I mentioned a few times, the Big 10 Conference was my primary obligation, while the Mid-American occupied much of my spare time. I was able to do some Horizon and Atlantic 10 games on occasion, but the volume of those games paled in comparison to the other conferences.

That being said, I felt very fortunate to be selected to work the league's Championship game despite not having done that many games in the conference. In their eyes, I was a 'part-timer', but they thought enough of my ability to give me the crown jewel game of the conference season. I was honored.

The game featured John Calipari's 22-6 Minutemen against John Chaney and his 17-11 Temple Owls. Lou Roe was the UMass leader, while Eddie Jones and Aaron McKie led the charge for Coach Chaney.

UMass used the home court advantage to cruise to a 69-61 win over the Owls. This game was the first of four straight times that Temple and UMass met in the A-10 Final. It was no secret that Calipari and Chaney weren't tremendous fans of each other, and it was this game that continued to stoke the fire between them. Just one year later, Chaney barged into a Calipari press conference and threatened to kick his ass and kill him.

I'm just glad Chaney wasn't having thoughts of butt kickings and homicides in 1991, when the game below happened.

#6) *Fit to be TIEd*

Temple vs West Virginia

Morgantown, WV

February 23, 1991

John Chaney had one of his better teams this season, led by the great Mark Macon. The Owls were 19-7 and headed to Morgantown to face Gale Catlett's 15-11 Mountaineers in their 1991 home finale. This was also my oldest daughter's 22nd birthday. I almost passed on this game for that reason.

Anybody that knows Coach Chaney knows how passionate and animated he was. Typically in a loose fitting vest and undone tie, Chaney gets your attention very quickly with his fiery demeanor. Coach did a heck of a job at Temple with his match-up zone, getting the most of his players.

With two games to go in the Atlantic 10 season, Temple and Rutgers were tied for the top spot in the conference standings. Assuming both teams won out, there would be a tie for the conference title.

In Morgantown that day, the fans were fired up. Not only was it Senior Day, but it was also the only time Coach Chaney would come to town. They were ready for him…signs everywhere, giant photo cut outs of Chaney's head, you name it. I'm sure Temple was used to this sort of treatment, but when you mix in the stakes of the game, tensions were amplified. Add to the equation, their best player, Mark Macon, wasn't going to play due to a sprained ankle.

The game started pretty typically, but shortly thereafter, it was obvious that it was going to be one of those days that the Owls just weren't going to have it. There were a few calls in the first half that were bang-bang type plays that ended up going against the Owls. The staff started to get a little mouthy and visibly perturbed, most notably, Coach Dean Demopoulos, who was Chaney's right-hand man. For whatever reason, Coach Demopoulos and I never did see eye to eye from the very beginning when I started doing Temple games. Maybe he just doesn't like Italians. Who knows.

With a minute to go in the first half and the Owls down 30, the ball went out of bounds. During that stoppage in play, Demopoulos made a smart remark to me. I had had enough of him and was tired of hearing it from that guy.

Boom. I gave him a technical and pointed right at him.

Coach Chaney immediately did a 2 ½ gainer off the bench and came flying out at me. To say he was furious wouldn't do the word 'furious' proper justice.

"YOU SON OF A BITCH!" he screams.

"What did you say?" I asked.

"YOU SON OF A BITCH!" he yells louder.

"That's what I thought you said," I replied.

I have some thick skin, but I'm not going to let him talk to me like that.

I'm pretty fired up at this point too since the Temple staff was riding us all game. I could give him a technical too, or I could throw his ass out and not have to hear it anymore. The second choice seemed like the way to go.

So, after I made him confirm what he said, I started my wind up to send Coach to the showers. If you can picture this, I leaned over and began the wind up with my hand down by my knees. As I started my upward motion, he was still very close to me. Too close.

As I brought my hand up at about 100 mph, my index finger caught the end of his tie. I yelled, "YOU'RE OUTTA HERE" and completed the motion to throw him out, and promptly smacked him in the face with his own tie.

Uh oh.

Completely accidental. But now, Coach was at an all-time high in rage. I'm sure he wanted to kill me. They were holding him back to get him to try and calm down. If he was a cartoon character, there would be bucket loads of steam coming out of his nose and his ears.

Still, after all this, I was still pretty angry at how they were treating us and for the scene that Chaney was making. It was out of control. He was undermining us and making a mockery of the situation. It seemed like a good idea at the time, so I yelled to those that were holding him back to let him go. What was he going to do—take a swing in front of 15,000 people?

Things finally settled as we went to the scorer's table to report all that happened. Once done, I was SUPPOSED to walk to the other side of the floor to help diffuse the situation. Nope. I was still fired up. I went and stood under the basket that Coach had to walk by in order to get to the locker room.

Chaney finally starts off toward the locker room with a

police escort. He stopped under the basket and we started going at it. Nose to nose. He was already tossed, so now he was going to get his money's worth. I didn't care. I gave it right back to him. What's he going to do, throw ME out??

After what seemed like three hours (probably more like 15 seconds), Morgantown's finest finally got Coach off the floor and into the locker room. The game resumed, and it was all West Virginia, to the tune of a 91-66 final.

The game was on a Saturday. The next Monday, I was at school preparing for the day when I got called to the office. There was a phone call for me from the Atlantic 10 Commissioner, Ron Bertovich. Ugh. I thought I was done in the A-10, and the commish was going to tell me that my services were no longer needed.

Instead, it was 3-way call, with John Chaney as the other participant. Both the Commissioner and Chaney apologized for the incident on behalf of the Atlantic 10. It was a classy gesture by both individuals. Normally the commissioner will take the back of the coaching icon, but he didn't. In turn, Chaney couldn't have been better. I also apologized for being out of line. Bygones were bygones at that point. The hatchet was buried.

A few days later, I received a letter in the mail from Coach Chaney once again apologizing for his "despicable behavior." I know games get intense, but it takes a real class act to apologize…TWICE…for an incident in a ball game. Coach gained a lot of respect from me by reacting the way he did.

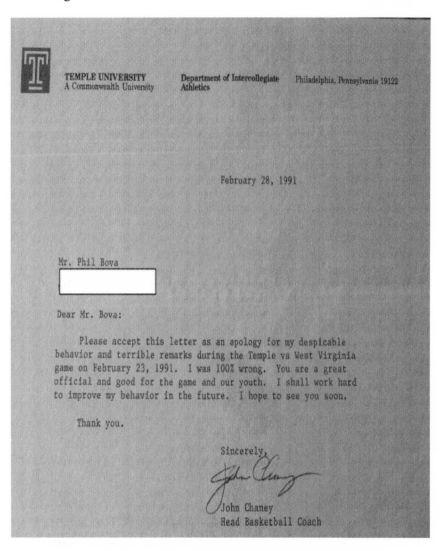

TEMPLE UNIVERSITY
A Commonwealth University

Department of Intercollegiate Athletics

Philadelphia, Pennsylvania 19122

February 28, 1991

Mr. Phil Bova

Dear Mr. Bova:

Please accept this letter as an apology for my despicable behavior and terrible remarks during the Temple vs West Virginia game on February 23, 1991. I was 100% wrong. You are a great official and good for the game and our youth. I shall work hard to improve my behavior in the future. I hope to see you soon.

Thank you.

Sincerely,

John Chaney
Head Basketball Coach

Apology letter from the Great John Chaney. All Class

#5) *Farewell St. John Arena*

Penn State vs Ohio State

Columbus, OH

February 28, 1998

The Buckeyes were concluding a historically bad season. It was so bad that they actually lost 17 straight games in a row. As competitive as the Big 10 generally is, 14 of those losses came within conference play. Freshman Michael Redd was on that squad, but he didn't have much help. The Nittany Lions had a decent season going and would eventually make it to the Finals of the NIT.

The close of this particular season in Columbus was a little different. This was the final game at St. John Arena. OSU was scheduled to make the move down the street to the Schottenstein Center for the 1998-99 campaign.

Growing up in Cleveland, I had seen and read about so many games in that arena. Since it opened in 1956, St. John Arena has seen great players, Big 10 Championship teams, and the 1960 National Champion. Some of my favorites like Lucas and Havlicek called this place home, and this was the last regular season game for the arena.

Ohio State played with passion, trying to send the old arena into retirement on a happy note by taking a 39-36 lead. At halftime, Ohio State brought back and introduced over 100 former players that built the legacy of St. John. The biggest ovation was for Coach Fred Taylor who was confined to a wheelchair and was the last coach to lead the Buckeyes to a national title. It was an emotional time for the players and fans to be sure.

Onto the second half, Ohio State led by eight points with about six minutes to play but couldn't hold it. After trading baskets in the final minutes, the game headed to overtime, tied at 76 apiece.

The extra session belonged to Penn State as a couple 3-pointers stretched a lead that Ohio State couldn't overcome. Despite 32 points from Michael Redd, Penn State prevailed 89-85.

I knew all season long that this game would be the last one at St. John Arena, and truthfully, it was a game that I really wanted to do. I was more than honored to be chosen to ref this game. The result of the game was meaningless in the scheme of things, but I will always be a part of history for the final game at St. John Arena. That's something I will always be proud of.

#4) *The 12 Year Story*

Ohio State vs Michigan State

Columbus, OH

January 10, 1987

Texas vs Michigan State

San Juan, PR

November 27, 1999

This memory is a 2-parter, with the second game happening 12 years later. The first half of the equation has to do with Gary Williams and the Buckeyes going to old Jenison Fieldhouse to take on Jud Heathcote's Spartans. Both teams were in the middle of the Big 10 pack at the time, but this game happened to be on national television.

It was a typical Big 10 game…very physical and a lot of calls in both directions. As you can imagine, both Williams and Heathcote were in rare form in working the officials to try and gain some kind of competitive advantage. Williams was usually very volatile, but he was particularly fired up that day.

Right before a television time out, an Ohio State player drove the lane and crashed into a Spartan as the ball went in the bucket. My partner had the call (I was on the opposite side), and he signaled a player control foul. Of course, that means foul on Ohio State, no basket, and we are going the other way.

The horn goes off. Television time out. Williams is ready to go. Here he comes out on the floor…headed toward my partner. Meanwhile, the players are also on the floor, sitting on those portable chairs. I knew this might get ugly. I headed over and told my less experienced partner to walk away, as I would handle Williams.

I tried to go the soothing route…

"Gary, it was a tough call…could have gone either way, but I really think he made the right call," I explained.

"BS, Phil!! That was terrible!!! Awful call!!!"

I heard that stuff all the time. That didn't bother me at all. After further trying to explain the play, I had thought we were at the point where we could move on and play basketball. Williams then turned his back and walked toward his players who were waiting for him on the floor. At that point, he turned his head a little and yelled over to me for his kids to hear:

"Hey...FUCK YOU, PHIL!!!"

At first I thought about ignoring it and walking away. And then I thought about it. And then I thought about it a little more. I didn't even make the call. I tried to take the high road and calm him down when I thought it was the right call to begin with. I took a step to walk away and thought to myself, "wait.... Did he just tell me to F off? Oh no.....not dealing with that today, G."

I headed to the Ohio State huddle. Williams is in the middle of them all on one knee while they are listening to him in a semi-circle around him. I get closer to the huddle as some of the Buckeye kids start to look up. I got behind Williams and tapped him on the shoulder. He looked up at me, and I said the following:

"Hey Gary, fuck me?   FUCK YOU!"

Boom. Technical Foul.

Williams went nuts. He said that I couldn't do that. I pulled him aside and told him that if he had something to say, to say it to me in private. If he ever told me to go F myself in front of a bunch of kids, I would do the same.

"Say one more thing, and I'll throw your ass out."

Williams was tough...he was a real ball-buster to the officials. I don't think many referees would approach him in the manner that I did. In fact, I know that to be true as one of his assistants told me as much during the next television time out. He told me that Williams thought I was nuts and that he had never been approached like that. Good. Mission accomplished.

Darryl Johnson's 29 points outpaced the 29 scored by Dennis Hopson, and Michigan State pulled out a 90-80 victory.

Nearly 12 years later, I have the Michigan State / Texas game at a Puerto Rico Holiday Tournament. Judging by the date, it must have been a Thanksgiving celebration tournament.

Prior to the game, the crew and I said hello to the coaches and players during shoot around. We said hello to Tom Izzo and his staff and then headed to the Texas sideline to introduce ourselves. With the conferences I had, I never had the opportunity to do a game with Texas before.

I introduced myself and my partners and then went into my normal spiel. "We know you aren't going to agree with everything we do, but we'll give it our best shot" and so on. After I gave my monologue, a Texas coach took a step forward and in front of his staff and my crew, said:

"Hey Phil.....fuck me? FUCK YOU!"

That was the very same Ohio State assistant that pulled me aside over a decade earlier. It was absolutely hysterical. The best pregame laugh I think I have ever had.

As we walked away, my partners asked what was wrong with that guy!? He was ticked off, and we hadn't even thrown the ball up yet.

"Long story, guys…I'll tell you at halftime!" Absolutely

classic moment.

In case you're curious, Texas ended up taking down Sparty, 81-74.

#3) *Beginning of the Fab 5*

Michigan vs Notre Dame

South Bend, IN

February 2, 1992

There was a lot of hype surrounding the Michigan program for the start of the 1991-92 season. Coach Steve Fisher had put together one of the greatest recruiting classes in recent memory. Four of the top nine ranked high school seniors had committed to the Wolverines. Add a highly regarded fifth commitment from Texas, and the Fab Five was born. The quintet of Chris Webber, Jalen Rose, Juwan Howard, Jimmy King, and Ray Jackson were ready to take the college basketball world by storm.

Michigan started off the season at 13-5, with all five freshmen playing regularly. After 4 relatively easy wins, Michigan took #1 Duke to overtime before losing by three. That was the sort of coming out party for the team. If they could play the #1 Blue Devils with Christian Laettner, Bobby Hurley, and Grant Hill to a draw, they could certainly play with anyone.

These guys were different. They had the loose, overly baggy uniforms and wore black socks. They had a certain aura, or confidence, or swagger about them. It was just different than what all of us were used to. These guys were like rock stars in basketball uniforms.

On the other side, Notre Dame was struggling. The Irish limped into the game at 7-10 and were clearly struggling to adapt to Coach MacLeod's system after so many years of Digger Phelps. Notre Dame had just lost to Detroit Mercy the game before, and they were anxious to right the ship against the Fab Five.

My partners and I entered the game as we usually did. We did our normal pregame meeting, exchanged pleasantries with Fisher and MacLeod, and took the floor for this nationally televised game. We were all very aware of this Fab Five and were anxious to see what these guys were all about.

The introductions began prior to the game. We waited as the Notre Dame PA announcer introduced one of the freshmen…then the 2nd, and the 3rd, and a 4th….and then the 5th?? Coach Fisher decided to put his prized recruiting class on the floor—in the starting lineup—for the first time. It was unprecedented. To my knowledge, it was the first time five freshmen started together for a major college program. The Irish were led by LaPhonso Ellis and not a whole lot else. This game had the feeling that Michigan was REALLY going to announce themselves as major contenders.

The horn sounded and the 10 players took the floor. I had the game ball in my hand and waited near the center circle. Everyone then took their places, including the guys that were going to jump. As I approached them and was getting ready to toss the ball up, I knew in my mind that I was presiding over something special. The ball went up, and the legend of the Fab Five went into overdrive.

Michigan was on an extreme adrenaline rush and raced out

to a 30-13 lead in South Bend, en route to a 38-27 halftime lead. Notre Dame fought back valiantly and cut the lead to 54-50 with about six minutes left. The maize and blue kept their composure though, and the Irish could come no closer than five points the rest of the way. Michigan ended up winning the game, 74-65.

The interesting thing about this game...the Fab Five scored ALL 74 points. Nine players in total played for Michigan, but nobody else put the ball in the hole. How could you not be impressed by what these kids were able to do?

This game was the springboard for the team's season, and they eventually would make a deep run into March Madness. After getting by Ohio State in the Elite Eight, and Cincinnati in the Final Four, the Fab Five earned a rematch with Duke for the National Championship. This time was different, as Duke cruised to a 71-51 win.

#2) *Nose to Nose*

DePaul vs Cincinnati

Cincinnati, OH

February 20, 1992

Entering this game, Bob Huggins and the Bearcats were 19-3 and were ranked in the Top 20 in the country. Joey Meyer and the Blue Demons were having a fine season as well and brought a 16-6 mark to Fifth Third Arena. Both teams were at the top of the Great Midwest Conference, and the game was critical to determining the regular season champion.

The game was tight through the first half, as the 20 minute horn sounded with a 39-39 score. You could tell from the beginning that these conference rivals were playing with a little extra intensity due to the stakes involved.

In the second half, Cincinnati separated themselves a bit and took a commanding 11 point lead with only 4.39 left to play. From that point on, the Blue Demons began to chip away at the lead. Turnovers, mistakes, and bad shots were starting to doom the Bearcats. I could tell Huggins was getting increasingly frustrated as he saw his big lead slipping away.

DePaul grabbed the lead by one with just 17 seconds left to play. Nick Van Exel from Cincinnati took the ball to the baseline, had the chance to score, but got it stripped by DePaul's Howard Nathan. I signaled VERY CLEARLY that Nathan had gotten all ball and that there was no foul. As the ball hit the floor, I VERY CLEARLY pointed to the floor indicating that I saw that the ball was still in play. Nathan then grabbed the ball and threw it down the floor to kill the rest of the clock. Final: DePaul 71, Cincinnati 69.

Huggins went berserk. I made the right call, but he needed someone to blame as his team couldn't hold an 11 point lead with less than five minutes to go. He wanted to blame the outcome of the game on that last play, but clearly, they had kicked around the last five minutes and had no one to blame but themselves.

As the game ended, he ran across the floor toward me and got in my face over the last play of the game. I wanted to get off the floor—I couldn't have cared less who won the game and who didn't.

I tried to side step to the right, he went left to block me. I went left, he went right. It was clear that he wanted to make a

121

scene instead of going back to the locker room and coaching his team on how NOT to melt down at the end of a game. It was more important to him to look like the tough guy.

Bob Huggins, doing what he does

As he was screaming like a buffoon and saying some things that he probably shouldn't have, I told him to get out of the way or I was going to kick his ass. I didn't have to deal with this knucklehead…I just wanted to get out of the gym and head home.

We finally separated, but Huggins wouldn't let it go. He told the media that I needed to "do my job" among some other choice words. He also made mention that "I get paid to coach. They get paid to officiate."

Wow. Spoken like a true philosopher. Where else can you

find that sort of brilliant observation?

Huggins never communicated with me after the game or really ANY time after that confrontation. Instead, he decided to take shots at me and my officiating in his book, which I won't even dignify by mentioning it. Again, he mentioned that I needed to "do my job". Well coach, if you would have done yours while up 11, you probably wouldn't have been in that situation.

I know, I know…he's going to blame me, and I will blame him. All I can do is refer to the Cleveland Plain Dealer article that appeared the following day.

Here's what it said:

"Double breasted blazer flapping freely at his side, Huggins prodded and pleaded without reward last night as his 19th ranked Bearcats blew an 11-point lead in the last 4:39 to lose 71-69, to DePaul.

"Not once did Huggins break from his prowling, scowling, and howling to take a seat during the game, but he might have plenty of time to sit and watch his team in the future after bumping official Phil Bova in a heated exchange that punctuated the final frantic seconds.

"Huggins went off like a trick cigar after DePaul's Howard Nathan stripped Cincinnati's Nick Van Exel as he drove for a potential tying jumper with the clock running down.

"Bova indicated a clean steal as DePaul's Stephen Howard picked up the ball and threw it down court as time expired. Huggins tracked down Bova at midcourt and as the buzzer sounded, bumped him and went nose-to-nose in a tirade that ended only when Huggins was physically restrained.

"Huggins flare up placed an ugly ending on a matchup bathed in unsightly build up throughout the week."

Your honor, I rest my case.

#1) *The Chair*

Purdue vs Indiana

Bloomington, IN

February 23, 1985

It's a real shocker that this one was the most memorable of the bunch, right? February 23rd reared its head again…and to think, I almost didn't take this game because it was my daughter Shelly's 16th birthday.

Indiana lost the previous season in the Elite 8, so expectations were high as usual for Steve Alford, Bob Knight, and the Hoosiers. Entering the 1984-85 season, Indiana was the preseason #4 team in the country. On the other hand, not much was expected from Purdue as they were never ranked in the Top 25 all year. But, as we all know, when you put rival teams on the floor, nearly anything can happen. And it did.

Frustration was already high for Coach Knight entering the game. With a 14-9 record, the Hoosiers were nowhere near what was expected. During the pregame, my partners and I talked about the perfect storm of factors for this contest—a struggling Hoosier team, a frustrated coach, and a bad-blood rivalry game against the Boilermakers.

Just four minutes into the game, we called a foul on Steve Alford for a hold during a scramble for the ball. Coach Knight wanted a jump ball but didn't get it. He was angry—you could see it painted on his face. Less than a minute later, we called a foul on Marty Simmons, and Knight was getting hotter. Shortly after that foul, Purdue inbounded the ball, and I got Daryl Thomas for reaching over the Purdue player. That was six team fouls on Indiana in the first five minutes of the half. Knight turned a shade of red that was brighter than a stoplight.

He had to let off some steam, and he did so by cussing my partner up and down. Too much. Way too much. He sat down, but then kept going at it. We had to give him a technical foul. Maybe that's what he wanted? Sometimes coaches do that purposely to fire up their teams. We've seen that before.

As the floor cleared to prepare the 2-shot technical, Steve Reid from Purdue stepped to the line. My partner handed Reid the ball, as I stood near the half-court line. Just as Reid took possession, I could see Knight grab a chair out of the corner of my eye.

Oh no. This can't be good.

Then out of nowhere, Coach Knight took a chair and launched it across the floor. Thank God it went between Reid and the basket and did not hit anybody when hurled at full speed. It eventually came to rest on the other side of the floor.

Coach Knight expressing some frustration

Now, I have seen a lot of basketball games in my life and hundreds of meltdowns by coaches, but I sure as heck have never seen anything like this before. How do you prepare for something like this? What's the protocol? I may not have had perfect attendance in Referee School, but I'm pretty sure "what do you do if the coach throws a chair across the floor" wasn't covered.

Remember, Coach Knight is like a God in Bloomington. But still, our job as officials was to restore order as quickly as possible. Assembly Hall is packed to the rafters and fired up in support of their General. Knight himself is full of rage. The players kind of all stood around looking at each other wondering what was going to happen next.

Needless to say, we had to give Knight a second technical which carries an automatic ejection. Coach didn't want to leave

126

though. Now what? His assistant coaches and school officials started to gather around the floor.

My partner, Fred Jaspers, went to the scoring table to fill them in on what was going on. The Indiana Athletic Director sought me out and asked if we had ejected Knight. What other choice did I have? This was the easiest no-brainer ejection of my career.

My partner with the 'adios' thumb, while I look for anything else that could possibly happen

Meanwhile, Coach is still standing on the sidelines as the crowd started chanting, "Bob-by!! Bob-by!!" It was chaotic to say the least.

Things started to settle, but Knight remained there. What

127

else could we do at that point? We couldn't physically remove him from the game, right? The only power we had in our possession was the technical foul. So we gave him a third one.

After getting a few more choice words in, he finally headed toward the locker room. Strangely enough, it was the exact same path that the chair he threw took. The crowd was still fired up and even started throwing some things on the court. Mostly spare change, but there were odds and ends of things all over the place. I've joked in the past that it worked out pretty well for me, as I made an extra few bucks that night clearing the floor of the loose change.

The view from the scene of the crime...

We had to get the game going again. Coach Knight had earned three technical fouls, which resulted in now SIX free throws for Reid. I almost felt for the kid at that point. The crowd was belligerent, and he would be by himself on an island for SIX shots. How often does that happen? Reid was a 90% shooter and at minimum would likely give Purdue five points from the stripe.

Reid calmly knocked down the first two shots as I remained near the Indiana bench talking to the assistants and trying to get everyone to get back to some sort of normalcy. Reid missed the third, and then the fourth, and the fifth, as he was clearly feeling some pressure. He did make #6, which turned the original 11-6 lead for Purdue to 14-6.

From that point on, the next hour and a half resembled an actual basketball game as opposed to a 3-ring circus. Purdue went on to beat the Hoosiers, 72-63.

That's what is great about sports. On any given day, you may see something that has never been done before. I just happened to be front and center on the one of the most infamous coaching tirades in American sports history. If you would like to view the sequence of events, check out YouTube, with a title of "Bobby Knight throws Chair".

I ended up having Indiana again a week or so later that season. Coach Knight made no mention of the Purdue game that was still so fresh in everyone's mind. I guess I didn't expect him to. He was the General and didn't really care what you thought or how you felt about him.

BUT, as I mentioned earlier, he did come to my official's camp that summer. He spoke to the campers for three hours and refused an appearance fee for his time and effort. THAT was his way to tip his cap as if to say he "owed me one." I was grateful that he did that and was extremely appreciative that he went way over and above the call of duty. There are some guys like—Knight and Chaney—that exemplify the brotherhood amongst the coaches and officials, as we are all doing our best to work with the kids and give back to the game. It's unfortunate that one Bearcat can try and ruin the bunch.

"Hey Ref...does your wife know you're screwing us?"

9

You Better Have a Support System

I've said a number of times that the real key to success in this business is in having a support staff at home to keep the mothership heading in the right direction. For some that live the bachelor lifestyle, it isn't as critical. Those guys are able to live out of a suitcase while travelling from college town to college town without too much concern about what's happening on the home front. For those of us with a spouse and children, the dynamic is completely different. More often than not, those munchkins had a busier schedule than I did! And Thank God For Donna.

The concept of the support system was a major point of emphasis at my Referee's Camp. I did my best to strongly suggest that attendees had their ducks in a row before trying to embark on making this a career. The time away from home can be lengthy and at the most inopportune times, but you don't want your family to suffer in any way during your absence.

So then I thought, maybe there are some aspiring young men and women out there that are reading this book and want to get into the business. What would I tell them about their support at home? So then I thought more... I'M not the one who should be talking about being at home—it should come right from the person that lived it.

As I sipped on a little vino (hey, I'm Italian) on my back patio writing this, I called for Donna and asked her to pull up a chair. It's time for me to turn into the interviewer:

Donna, I'd like you to add some of your perspective on being the spouse of a college basketball referee.

DB: I'm glad you didn't pursue the NBA when you had the opportunity. You would have been gone way too much. You were gone a lot as it was.

Correct. Big difference between a 35 game college basketball season and 82 games in the NBA...

DB: Don't know how they do it. I'm pleased you were able to stay regional and not off to Phoenix and Miami every other night.

The NBA is a different animal. I wanted to talk a little about what we went through. The travel...the late nights...things like that.

DB: It was a Catch-22. With the per diem that you got to work each game, it became a decision of you flying some places to get in, out, and home quicker...versus driving some places and being able to put a few more bucks away for all your effort. It was on me to handle all the added responsibilities while you were away.

Short of experimenting with the Mantis, I drove as often as I could to save as much as possible.

DB: With all the money we spent on gas, I should have made you take the bus to Iowa City once in a while.

I guess the bus is better than making me ride my bike... Anyway, go back to the beginning. How hard is it to juggle everything until you establish a routine?

DB: You have to remember, we were married 5-6 years before you started getting serious in this basketball thing. And it was about 10 years before you joined the Big 10. At that point, when you started travelling more, we had three kids between the ages of three and six. Everything I did revolved around the kids.

Almost like being a single parent during hoops season...

DB: There were a lot of school functions that I went to by myself because of your travel. In reality, I didn't have much adult interaction because I was anchored to the house. By the time Michael was in 1st grade, I realized I needed to do something and ended up taking the test to become a Real Estate Agent. That was something I could do on MY schedule.

Besides helping the college fund, that was important?

DB: It was important to have something to do. For ME at least. Not sure about anyone else. If I didn't have an outlet or a hobby to occupy my time, I would have driven myself nuts. There's a lot of solo time to deal with between October and March. I'm just not the type of person to sit on the couch and watch *Law and Order* all night while you are gone.

Thank God for that...

DB: On the other hand, this arrangement really helped me be more of an independent person. You weren't around much for things like paying the bills, taking the kids to appointments, or helping around the house. Of course, I had to help with your career too. It was a challenge for sure, but I had the right mentality

133

about it all to make things go smoothly.

Did you even watch many of the games that I was doing when I had televised games?

DB: I would tune in when I could. The girls weren't big basketball fans, but your son definitely was. I remember him telling me that it was good that you had the kind of bald head that you did because it was easier to find you on the floor.

Bald is beautiful, honey.

DB: It was more difficult trying to explain to your son why some of the coaches were yelling "very bad words" in your direction.

I guess it isn't too often when you see one of your parents in a heated discussion while at work.

DB: It was harder taking the family to games. No matter if you are sitting in the home section or away section, most fans aren't going to applaud the officials for anything. The refs are always a target. I remember one game at Michigan State when a fan said something negative about you. Jennifer stood up, started wagging her finger in that guy's face and said, "That's my father you are talking about!!!" Pretty sure he didn't say much after that. People forget that you guys are human too with families.

I guess that's part of......

DB: And then there was that guy at Youngstown...stamping his feet the entire time and pointing his black umbrella at you everywhere you went. When I finally had the nerve to tell him to stop it and leave you alone, he said, "Why...are you his wife or something?" Ding, ding, Genius... I know people pay their money and can say whatever they want at a game, but you guys are doing your best. Don't they understand that?

I don't think they care. They just want their team to win by any means necessary.

DB: As much as I wanted to defend you, it was usually better that I kept my mouth shut and stayed anonymous. I did enjoy going to games, but I knew to bite my tongue most of the time.

It really helped when you came, because there were times I was too exhausted to drive back and you were able to help. Most of the time, I had to be ready to teach the next day.

DB: A long drive late at night with bad Midwest weather wasn't fun for me either. Remember the time we were coming back from Ohio State in the blizzard? It took FOREVER. I started driving and then woke you up to finish. We were both exhausted. A few hours later, I put the *Tarantella* (Italian song) on and we started dancing in the car to help wake us both up. Next thing you know...

Yep...sirens...

DB: A police officer pulls us over because he thought we were drunk. As much as you tried to explain that you just officiated a game and you were tired, he still wanted your license and registration. And coyly, you also handed him the card that mentioned you were a policeman's son.

Can't hurt, right?

DB: The officer came back and said he wasn't going to give us a ticket. After all, we didn't do anything wrong. Phil—do you remember what he said?

135

Not really...I think I was still half asleep..

DB: "You're a little too old to still be riding on your dad's coattails..."

Whatever. He probably wanted whoever was playing Ohio State to win that night. What else was difficult?

DB: I realize other women have husbands that travel a lot for a living, but the difference here is that the travel happened during the week AND on weekends. There was no time to 'catch up' on things with you. I had the day-to-day worries during the week and then was left out socially on the weekends. Sure, we would be invited to parties, dinners, etc., but I never wanted to go alone. Eventually those calls would be less and less as most people assumed you were out of town all the time. That was hard too. That's why it was important to have a job or outlet outside of the norm. Then during the spring and summer, you were around all the time and things were back to easy again.

See? You were actually fortunate...you had me DOUBLE the time during summer vacation and non-basketball months!

DB: Yep. Reeeeeeal fortunate.

I'm going to pretend that wasn't sarcastic. We are getting off track here. What advice would you give to the Basketball Widows of America when accepting a role in support of your spouse?

DB: You have to be strong. You have to be supportive of his/her career. You have to have TRUST. You have to have thin skin...not only with fans, but with commentators and newspapers. You have to be independent—able to handle your own needs, as well as any children you may have. Speaking of the children, they need to be on board too. Dad might not be there for every school play, band concert, or ball game, but they have to understand that it's for the greater good of the family. If you are able to get everyone on the same page and moving in the right direction, it can absolutely work.

Thanks Honey. I couldn't have done it without you.

DB: You're lucky to have me (wink).

Donna was absolutely right. My job was hard, but her job was harder. I was blessed from the Man Above to have a partner that was as fantastic as she was and, I was even further blessed to have a family that was as supportive as mine was. That's nothing to be taken for granted.

"Sir, I must respectfully disagree."

-Northwestern Student (probably on Debate Team)

10

The Big 10, well, actually 14

Quite often, I get asked what it's like to be on the floor in certain arenas, or how it is working with certain coaches. While I am most known for my time in the Big 10, I was fortunate to work games in a few other conferences as well. I mentioned the MAC earlier, but I was also able to work games for the Horizon League and the Atlantic 10 when it didn't conflict with my primary league.

I had Calipari at UMass, Chaney at Temple, Digger at Notre Dame, Coach K at Duke, Pitino at Kentucky among many others. I was lucky enough to work in so many great places outside of my conference during the non-conference portion of the schedule, as it was dependent upon which conference selected the officials to work the games. As an example, I worked at Cameron Indoor when Illinois played there… and since the Big 10 chose, I was working in ACC Country.

No matter the conference, the protocol was the same. The proper time to arrive at the arena, the pregame, and the time to be on the floor was all standard among fellow officials. One other thing I would like to mention was a protocol for every game I did.

Both teams warmed up on the floor up to 20-30 minutes prior to tip off and then retreated to the locker room for last minute instruction. It was customary for the captains of each team to meet at center circle with the referees during that warm up period. I always tried to make that meeting happen at exactly 13 minutes and 7 seconds prior to the opening tip.

Why 13:07? Simple. I mentioned earlier that my father was a detective in the Cleveland Police Department. My dad's badge was #307. Since 3:07 was too close to tip off time to have the captain's meeting, 13:07 was the next best alternative to have his badge number included in the timing of the meeting. That was my own personal tip of the cap to my role model as he was about to watch my game from heaven.

Remembering my father at 13:07 always gave me a sense of security and confidence.

Dad saw me work a number of beauties in the Big 10. Again, that's where I spent most of my time, and I have very vivid memories of those coaches and arenas. Every one of these venues had something special about them. You know for certain that if you were officiating a game in any of them, you were in for an intense night. Here are some of my personal thoughts and experiences at those schools during my 30 years from 1977-2006.

Illinois

Assembly Hall

Memorable Players: Derek Harper, Nick Anderson, Kendall Gill

Memorable Coaches: Lou Henson, Bill Self

I always liked Assembly Hall in Champaign (now State Farm Center). Assembly Hall opened in the 1960s and was the largest dome structure in America prior to the Houston Astrodome. It held somewhere in the neighborhood of 16,000 people and was always packed to the rafters. Great venue for college hoops.

Champaign wasn't the easiest to get to. I'd either take a flight to Chicago and drive the two hours down, or if time allowed, would make the six hour drive. Either way, it was a project for me to do a game for the Illini.

The Illinois students were always very active. They called themselves the "Orange Krush" and were very much in tune with the game and were relentless to the officials. Every once in a while, I would look in their direction, give them a wink, and tell them, "Yeah, yeah…I hear ya…" Sometimes that little wink might buy me some mercy and make them think, "Maybe that Bova isn't such a bad guy afterall!" As far as the band goes, the "Illini War Chant" was always played prior to tip off. That's a tradition that the University ended in 2017.

140

Illinois was fortunate to have two really outstanding coaches who are both Hall of Famers in Lou Henson and Bill Self. Henson liked to wear that orange blazer at home games that I always liked. He was always tough on me—very demonstrative with throwing his hands in the air and making a scene. More than a couple times, I would run by Lou, and he made sure he got a few words in.

Self parlayed a few great seasons in Champaign to a highly successful career at Kansas. I remember one time specifically that he called me out during a time out and said, "Phil—eight fouls on us, only two on them?!?" I asked him to check the tape and get back to me. Wouldn't you know it, a week later, I received a card in the mail from Bill Self. It read something like this:

"I checked the tape. Out of the eight calls, seven were correct and you blew the 8th. You're not as perfect as you think you are!"

Of course, the last line was in jest, but he did want to bust my hump a little. He is a good guy and a good coach that I have a lot of respect for.

Illinois was always in the top half of the standings, winning the conference title a few times. Of course, the 2004-05 team that started 29-0 and finished 37-2 with Deron Williams, Luther Head, and Dee Brown really stands out. That team made it to the NCAA Finals and lost to North Carolina, 75-70.

Indiana

Assembly Hall

Memorable Players: Isiah Thomas, Steve Alford, Calbert Cheaney

Memorable Coaches: Bob Knight

Assembly Hall (Indiana's version) was probably THE most iconic arena in the Big 10. The rafters were dripping with history since its opening in 1971. You could count on 17,000+ every night whether the Hoosiers were playing hated rivals Purdue and Notre Dame or The Little Sisters of the Poor. In fact, famed basketball announcer Gus Johnson agrees with me, calling Assembly Hall the "Carnegie Hall of Basketball." The design of the arena is definitely unique as there are only 20 rows behind the basket, while the sideline views to the top rows are very steep. A 2012 poll ranked Assembly Hall as the third best home court advantage—ranking just below Allen Fieldhouse in Kansas and Cameron Indoor at Duke. GREAT place for college basketball.

Bloomington, Indiana was also a bit of a haul for me, as it was about five and a half hours by car....or an all-night adventure when travelling in the winter with The Mantis!

In 2016, USA Today ranked the IU student section as sixth best in the country. The University allows for 7,800 seats for students, which was easily the largest in the country. The same report claims that Roy Williams once said that he wished the Dean Smith Center sounded like Assembly Hall did.

Of course, you can't think about Indiana Basketball without thinking about Bobby Knight. Coach Knight started at Indiana at the same time Assembly Hall opened, which of course linked them forever. There was always something special watching the Indiana kids trot out there for warmups in their horizontal crimson and cream striped pants and script Indiana on their tops. I loved that. It was classy, but also with a nod to history.

Some coaches came out during the warmups to chat with the officials and see how their kids looked during the pregame. Not Coach Knight. Every time that I can remember, the Indiana kids would warm up and we would have our captain's meeting at 13:07. The kids would continue to warm up and then head to the locker room for last minute pregame preparation. They would return to the floor to put a few more shots in the air, and then with a minute to go, the buzzer would sound for the players to head to the bench for introductions.

As the buzz started to intensify in anticipation of the game about to begin, out of nowhere, you could hear a roar that sounded like a jet engine was about to take off. Why?

Here. Comes. Knight.

Coach would make his grand entrance to the bench at the last minute and the place would go NUTS. He was like Elvis entering the building. He strolled onto the floor and walked directly into his huddle. After the introductions, he would shake the other coach's hand. If he liked you as a referee, he would come say hello. If he didn't, you just got the Knight Death Stare and he walked right by you. He tried to intimidate before the game even started. On several occasions, I made sure I was facing the other direction when he came out so that I wouldn't be caught in his web.

Indiana has had a tremendous amount of success over the years, winning the conference title six times during my 30 years. Certainly, there were tremendous players like Isiah Thomas and Steve Alford and great story lines with Coach Knight. Mix in great success including a couple National Championships in 1981 over North Carolina and the Keith Smart winner in 1987 over Syracuse, and you have the key components of one of the nation's truly elite basketball programs.

Only at Indiana could I experience the following... On March 12, 1994, I had the Wisconsin/Indiana game. It was Senior night, and Assembly Hall was packed as usual. What better way to say thank you to the fans, friends, and families than to have a ceremony during the final home game.

As Coach Knight shares his closing thoughts to the Hoosier faithful, he uncorks this memorable poem:

"When my time on earth is gone

And my activities here are passed,

I want they bury me upside down,

And my critics can kiss my ass."

Ladies and Gentlemen, Bob Knight.

Iowa

Carver Hawkeye Arena

Memorable Players: Ed Horton, Acie Earl, Andre Woodridge

Memorable Coaches: Lute Olson, Tom Davis

Carver-Hawkeye didn't look like much from the outside, but they packed in 15,000+ for ball games in Iowa City. The arena must have been built into the ground a bit, as it didn't look as palatial from the outside. The inside was gorgeous though. Even though Iowa is more of a football and wrestling school, they did a great job with the basketball program.

So, what's the easiest way to get to Iowa City from Cleveland? Hint: there isn't one. An eight hour drive straight west didn't sound like much fun, so I typically flew to Chicago, connected to Cedar Rapids, and then drove the last half hour to Iowa City. Needless to say, I didn't do any games on a weeknight in Iowa City when there was school the next day. I would have needed a rocket to get back home on time.

Iowa's student section was called the "Iowa Hawk's Nest." They were great. Since there isn't a whole lot to do in Iowa other than milk cows or shuck corn, they supported the school teams with a lot of spirit. Maybe it was the black and gold color scheme that the crowd dressed to, but I often thought it was a tough place to play. Many of the kids would wear overalls with black and gold vertical stripes...it was a fun atmosphere.

I really liked Lute Olson early on. He was always dressed impeccably and had that silver fox/GQ look about him. Rarely did he lose control of his emotions. Of course, George Raveling, Dr. Tom Davis, and Steve Alford had stints in Iowa City during my time. They were all great coaches. Let's be honest--Iowa City isn't going to be confused with any major metropolis. To get that high quality coaching AND recruit good kids to play in Iowa City was no small task. It shows what the impact of a strong athletic department can have on the fortunes of a school. They just did things right.

To that point, even the folks in Iowa knew how difficult it was to get in and out of campus. The good people at Iowa set up police escorts for us to leave after the game. We would get to our rental cars, follow the police to the highway, and they would give us a 'thumbs up' as we passed through all the traffic. It was actually kind of funny to listen to Dr. Tom complain about us routinely on the radio as we left town. So on second thought, maybe they weren't trying to be nice…maybe they were just trying to prevent three homicides.

The Hawkeyes always had solid teams. They had excellent coaching and a hard-working Midwest mentality from the kids. You didn't see too many 5-star recruits land in Iowa City, but you always saw good TEAM basketball. I'm pretty sure they didn't win the conference at any point during my run, but they were almost always in the mix. Any team playing in Iowa City knew they were going to have their hands full that night.

Michigan

Crisler Center

Memorable Players: Glen Rice, Fab Five, Robert Traylor

Memorable Coaches: Bill Frieder, Steve Fisher

The Crisler Center at Michigan was built in the late 1960s, and for a school of its size, is one of the smaller Big 10 arenas, holding around 13,000 people. Very clearly, Michigan is much more of a football school with the Big House next door holding over 100,000 fans. Maybe they ran out of seats to put inside of Crisler. The design was a giant bowl…or flying saucer, and they were right on top of you.

I was fortunate enough to do a lot of games at Michigan because it was easy for the Supervisor of Officials to place me there. Besides Columbus, Ann Arbor was the closest Big 10 city to me. I could easily make the couple hour drive during the week and be in bed at a decent hour for school the next day.

The students at Michigan were right on top of the floor; you can always see them dressed in their finest maize shirts on TV. They called themselves the "Maize Rage" and took themselves very seriously. They had a board, a constitution, AND a dress code. With me being from Ohio, you can rest assured that they let their feelings toward me be known! For whatever reason, they ALWAYS knew when I would be doing their games.

One of my favorite coaches during my entire time as an official was Steve Fisher. I can't say enough positive things about him—always upbeat and very positive toward his players and toward all of us wearing stripes. One of the things he said to me that I will never forget was, "Phil…I tolerate most officials-YOU, I respect." Total class act.

Big fan of Coach Fisher

Tommy Amaker was another coach that was very respectful to us and the game. I'm a big fan of his and hope that he continues to do well.

The Wolverines had solid teams during the Roy Tarpley and Gary Grant era, but it was Glen Rice and Rumeal Robinson that led the team to a National Championship in 1989. Shortly thereafter, the Fab Five arrived in Ann Arbor and really turned the football school into a 2-sport powerhouse. As aforementioned, I officiated the first Fab 5 game (with all five freshmen starting) against Notre Dame.

Hail, hail, Michigan.

Michigan State

Breslin Center

Memorable Players: Magic Johnson, Scott Skiles, Mateen Cleaves

Memorable Coaches: Jud Heathcote, Tom Izzo

The Jack Breslin Center came into existence in the mid-1980s, replacing the old Jenison Fieldhouse. Moving to the newly created Breslin Center gave Sparty an increase in capacity from roughly 10,000 seats to around 16,000. Little known fact about the Breslin Center... The university purchased the actual floor used during the 2000 Final Four (and championship win over Florida) and installed it at the Breslin Center. There is a plaque on the floor near the Michigan State tunnel commemorating the championship. That's pretty cool.

I did a bunch of games in East Lansing, too many to count honestly. Similar to their in-state neighbors, Michigan State was another venue I could be assigned to regularly due to the proximity to Cleveland. This was one place you really had to have your game face on from the opening tip. I loved doing games there as it was as intense there as any arena in the country.

The same USA Today report that listed Indiana having the sixth best student section lists Michigan State's Izzone as the fourth. "The Izzone" was 4,000 people strong with seats in both the upper and lower bowls of the arena. I heard that the lower bowl seats require students to camp out over night to get them, so you bet your bottom dollar they get their money's worth on game day. Everyone wears white and is as involved in the game as any student section in the country. The Izzone first started as the Spartan Spirits under Coach Heathcote, and they seemingly get stronger every year. I guess Big 10 Championships and National Championships will do that for you.

Both Spartan coaches are iconic in the game of college basketball. Jud Heathcote was a very tough customer and always gave you that look like he was sucking on a lemon. He had won the Big 10 title three times, two of which came in his first couple years. It's often said that the popularity of college basketball exploded after the 1979 title game between Michigan State and Indiana State. Any basketball fan knows that was the Magic Johnson / Larry Bird game. Well, Jud was front and center then and helped put Michigan State firmly on the map.

One of my favorite incidents in East Lansing was during a time out. Jud had the sourpuss face on and continued bending my ear, as he had been all half. I was getting to the point where I wasn't going to take any more. Rather than call him out during the time out, I motioned to his assistant to come see me. A young guy

149

named Tom Izzo.

"Hey, Tommy—you want to be a head coach in this league someday, right?" I asked him.

"Yes, sir, you bet I do," Izzo replied.

"Well, you will be in about 2 minutes if Jud doesn't get his shit together because I am going to throw his ass out. You go tell him I said that."

Speaking of Izzo, he has become the Dean of the Big 10 coaches. He was an assistant under Jud for 13 years and then took the program to the next level. I have often said that teams take on the personality of their coaches, and there is no better example than Michigan State. Izzo is a tough, no nonsense guy, and his teams play the same way. When I have one of Izzo's games, I know it's going to be a tough, physical contest. Tom's record and success in tournaments speak for themselves. Michigan State is truly blessed to have these two lead the program for over 40 years.

Tom Izzo when he was the REAL head coach!

Michigan State is always in the running for conference honors and to make noise in the NCAA tournament. The players they have had from Magic to Skiles to Steve Smith to Mateen Cleaves and a strong leader…with a healthy dose of the Izzone make Sparty a tough game no matter where you play them.

Minnesota

Williams Arena

Memorable Players: Kevin McHale, Randy Breuer, Willie Burton

Memorable Coaches: Jim Dutcher, Clem Haskins

Williams Arena (also known as The Barn) in Minneapolis is the oldest venue in the Big 10, having been built in 1928. It's also the arena with the most distinctive features. The roof is an arched design which looks like an airplane hangar. The playing surface is raised off the actual floor by two feet, so team benches and the scoring tables are actually below the court. In reality, players and fans on the first floor are viewing the game from knee level. Other than players in the game and the officials, the only other person allowed on the court is the head coach. Williams clearly has a unique design, but this awesome arena stays firm to its historic roots in the 1920s.

I didn't do as many games in Minneapolis as I did most other places, as Williams Arena was a 'weekend only' game for me. I never was too interested in making the 11 hour journey by car, as the Gophers were the farthest destination for me.

What good is "The Barn" without "The Barnyard"? The student section at Minnesota affectionately calls themselves The Barnyard. Because of the unique design of the arena, and its resemblance to a giant barn, the nicknames to both were a natural. Many of the students in the section dressed in over the top costumes that were usually in some reference to a farm animal. The Barn is a bit cavernous, so it didn't typically get too loud in there. That said, it was pretty common for me to get cackled at by chickens, cows, and some of Ol' McDonald's finest. I do remember telling a pig in the stands during a time out that "I eat bacon for breakfast," and smiled at myself as I walked away.

Early on in my career, I had the good fortune of working with Jim Dutcher on a number of occasions. Without question, he was the consummate professional—one of the true good guys in the game. Coach Dutcher was the last coach for the Gophers to win the Big 10 regular season, having done so in 1981-82 with Randy Breuer and Trent Tucker. That was no small accomplishment with the other giants in the league. I particularly enjoyed Clem Haskins as well. Just like their counterparts in Iowa City, recruiting to the northernmost city in the Big 10 with a facility that was from the 1920s was a tough sell. I had great respect for those guys for being as competitive as they were.

I never knew where they found these guys, but they always had giant white guys patrolling the paint. Guys like the 7'3" Randy Breuer and 6'10" Kevin McHale. Size like that is pretty common in today's game, but not nearly as much back in the decades of the 80s and 90s. Big hulking guys, but always very respectful. There were a couple times these giants knocked me into the band...right into the tuba section. The crowd started clapping, the coaches were laughing—just one of those times you hoped that the cameras weren't rolling. When I saw my partner during the timeout, he said, "You're having a hard enough time on the floor, the last thing we need is for you to join the band. You'll clear this place out in a heartbeat." He was right. I didn't know a tuba from a hole in the ground.

The Gophers were very typically a middle of the pack program. Some good years, some bad. Made the tournament on occasion, but usually had a better chance of making the NIT. In this day and age of luxury suites and basketball palaces, walking into Williams and doing a game was always special. It wouldn't have surprised me if there were still some peach baskets nailed to the wall in the side gym.

Northwestern

Welsh-Ryan Arena

Memorable Players: Geno Carlisle, Evan Eschmeyer

Memorable Coaches: Rich Falk, Bill Carmody

Welsh-Ryan Arena opened in 1952 and is the smallest venue in the Big 10, holding only about 8,000 fans for Wildcat basketball. I always found it a bit strange that the school that is located nearest the biggest city had the smallest arena. Then again, Northwestern is known much more for its Medill School of Journalism and academics than its prowess on the hardcourt. Different priorities I suppose.

Evanston, Illinois is just north of Chicago. This was another school that was typically a weekend game for me. I made that five and a half hour drive on occasion, but it was a real bear to get back after the game. Luckily there were several flights between Chicago and Cleveland, and that was generally the path I took.

I really don't particularly remember much about the student

section. They got on us like all schools do, but there wasn't anything that really stood out. Maybe they were sitting there devising mathematical equations to get in our heads somehow. One incident did stand out.

We were doing a game at Evanston, and the game was being televised on ESPN2. There were five students near the front that sat there with their shirts off, and each had a letter painted on their chest. The first had an "E", the second had an "S", and so on until the 5th student had a "2". Well, the last guy, the "2" had a mouth on him that would embarrass any drunken sailor. He cussed non-stop at me….the players…heck, even the popcorn guy.

During a time-out, I asked him to tone it down, as that behavior would not be tolerated. Yes, I know, he bought his ticket and he should be able to say what he wants, but there is a line that should not be crossed. He kept going and going. I gave him a final warning that told him that enough is enough and if he continued, he would be watching the rest of the game from the parking lot.

He didn't take me seriously.

During the next TV timeout, I walked over to the nearby police officer and told him about the situation. I asked that he remove Mr. #2 so the game could continue. I wasn't going to deal with this moron all night.

The officer did as I asked and removed him from his seat. It was clear to me that he WANTED to be on display and get all the attention he could, so I purposely tossed him during a time out when the cameras were away and fans weren't paying attention. He took his 1-man comedy show to the next watering hole, I'm sure. In the meantime, the game continued.

I looked back at the empty seat, and his four buddies next to him. At that point, I realized that I had just taken this game from ESPN2 to ESPN, because the 2 was thrown out on his ear. If I had the time and energy, I would have loved to have drawn a chalk outline on that chair where that yo-yo used to sit until he met his demise with me.

On the coaching front, Rich Falk was a heck of a player, but had a hard time drawing top talent to Evanston. There were several coaches over the three decades that I recalled. Kevin O'Neill was there for a few years, and that guy was crazy. Maybe that's why we got along so well as I was just as nuts as he was. Bill Carmody had a long run there as well, but he was a pain in my backside every time I had him. Maybe he tried to overcompensate with the officials to help overcome the usual talent discrepancy. The Northwestern coaches had a tough job. Selling Chicago was easy, but selling a 'high school' size gym with high academic standards was difficult. The elite players weren't going to go there. They had to make the program work with less than perfect players, but they always played as a team.

From a personnel standpoint, the Wildcats had a few guys that made all Big 10 honors, but that was few and far between. My perception of Northwestern is that they were tough as heck at home. They would fight, scratch, and claw you to death. You had better not take the night off when going to Northwestern as they were still good enough to knock you off if you didn't come to play.

In general, Northwestern struggled and almost always finished at the bottom of the conference. They never challenged for any league titles, and they didn't even make the NCAA tournament until well after I retired from the game. Truth be told, I have often thought that Northwestern could be a sleeping giant when it comes to Big 10 hoops.

Ohio State

St. John Arena

Schottenstein Center

Memorable Players: Clark Kellogg, Jimmy Jackson, Greg Oden

Memorable Coaches: Gary Williams, Thad Matta

Being an Ohio guy, I always enjoyed reffing games in Columbus. The first 20 or so years of my career with Ohio State was in cozy St. John Arena. That place opened in 1956 and was the home of the Buckeyes for just over four decades. It held just over 13,000 folks and had a lot of character to it as most arenas built in the 50s did.

As basketball's popularity rose, so did the TV dollars and the need for luxury suites. The Buckeyes moved to the Schottenstein Center, which is as beautiful as any arena in the country. This palace is the largest in the Big 10, holding nearly 19,000 people at capacity. While gorgeous, I really felt that the old St. John Arena actually gave the Buckeyes a better home court advantage. "The Schott" is almost like a professional arena and probably the nicest arena I ever worked in.

I did dozens of games in Columbus, as it was only a couple hour drive down I-71 for me. Weekdays and weekends were no problem for me, and the Supervisor of Officials knew that. It was an easy call for him to send me to Columbus.

Action shot with Ohio State's Perry Carter

"The Buckeye Nuthouse" was the section for the student faithful. I never did understand the placement of the students behind the baskets (they were moved to behind the benches and behind the opposing second half basket in 2009). The students didn't have as much of an impact as they did at other places like Michigan State and Indiana. There was more of a high-ticket price / corporate crowd near the sidelines, and that was good for the officials. It was twice as unlikely to be called the names I did by owners of companies than I was by some college kid after a few beverages.

I started with Eldon Miller who was a laid back, professional guy. Gary Williams was just the opposite—very fiery and intense, as I had shared earlier. Thad Matta was another coach I enjoyed working with. He was very similar to Miller, but actually a very funny guy when you talked to him one on one. I worked with five different guys in Columbus, but the program was always in good hands.

It seemed that Ohio State always had at least one star on their hands...starting with Clark Kellogg and going through guys like Dennis Hopson, Jimmy Jackson, Michael Redd, and Greg Oden. They were always very athletic, so you knew you had to be at your best to keep up and see everything that was going on.

The Buckeyes were typically a middle to upper middle of the conference team. They had good success in the early 90s with Jim Jackson's group and won a couple conference titles and then came back to life with Matta, Oden, and Conley. Ohio State is a football dominant school like the team from up north, but definitely has the ability and facility to be a national power every year.

Penn State

Bryce Jordan Center

Memorable Players: John Amaechi, Matt Gaudio, Joe Crispin

Memorable Coaches: Jerry Dunn, Ed DeChellis

I was thrilled to see Penn State join the Big 10 in 1990. It made perfect sense for them to leave the Independent ranks and join a power conference like the Big 10. Plus, it gave the conference a needed presence in Pennsylvania. The Lions broke ground on Bryce Jordan a couple years after joining the Big 10 and moved from the old Rec Hall to Bryce Jordan in 1996.

They did a heck of a job on that arena in Happy Valley. It

holds about 15,000 for hoops and is used for a multitude of purposes. Since it was fairly new compared to its counterparts in the Big 10, it had a lot more bells and whistles than the others. It was similar to Ohio State, but not as big.

State College was- no man's land for me. It was a four hour drive…which isn't TOO far, but almost not far enough to fly. That's what made weeknight games a real challenge. And, that's why I experimented with Craig Kuhn. Weather was always a concern in making that trip east. I didn't get placed there too often during the week, but it certainly made for a long night when heading back home after a 7 o'clock tipoff.

Penn State is legendary for the support from students. The 'white out' for football is one of college's best scenes. Basketball started to catch up. In the early 2000s, they started a student group called the "Nittwits" (obviously a play on "Nitt"any Lions). Like their brethren in Evanston, the Lions hoops program struggled to be successful, which made it difficult to get the student support that the football team received. In fact, Coach Paterno would sometimes sit near the top to watch games, and it was like St. Peter was watching from Heaven. The Lion fans seemed to be more interested in seeing JoePa than what was happening on the floor.

The three coaches I had the pleasure of working with were class individuals, but again, fought the same issues that Northwestern had. It was difficult to win at a program with very little history (and a football school), and consequently, the frustration level would boil over at times. I understood that.

From a player standpoint, Penn State never produced a REAL superstar during my three decades. Some solid guys that made it to the next level, but no one really stood out. Again, I make the comparison to Northwestern…solid, fundamental teams

159

that could beat you if you didn't come to play.

I believe the Lions made the NCAA tournament twice during that time frame and actually finished as high as second once in the conference in 1995-96. This is another sleeping giant.

Purdue

Mackey Arena

Memorable Players: Joe Barry Carroll, Glenn Robinson, Cuonzo Martin

Memorable Coaches: Gene Keady

Unlike the last two schools, Purdue was a basketball school first and foremost. Mackey Arena in West Lafayette, Indiana, was built in 1967 and was renovated a number of times, but it still holds somewhere in the neighborhood of 14,000+ fans. The domed, aluminum roof is what makes Mackey different as the noise level is tremendous. John Feinstein once said, "When the Boilermakers are on a run, you literally can't hear the guy next to you talking." I believe it.

Most of my games at Purdue were on weekends or during the week if Buckeye was on Christmas Break. A five hour drive in the middle of winter didn't sound like much fun, so I normally flew to Indianapolis and then drove the final hour to West Lafayette.

Purdue students were into it. They had the "Gene Pool" when Coach Keady was there, and it eventually morphed into the "Paint Crew" for Coach Painter. There was something about walking out of that tunnel and being immersed into that sea of

Black and Old Gold. It was impressive. And the fans were jacked up. It was almost as if someone pressed a button right before tip-off and the intensity level went right through that aluminum roof. Great place to watch a game.

Gene Keady was the head coach for 25 of the 30 years I did Purdue games and was eventually succeeded by Matt Painter. Keady was a classic. He and I got along great, but he always gave you that scowl like he had bad gas. He loved that comb over look too…I used to joke that he combed his hair with a rake. Keady knew that he walked on water at Purdue and also knew that all he had to do was stand up, flail his arms, and give that gassy look for the crowd to get all fired up. He knew how to work it. Still, I have a lot of respect for him. I asked him to come to my camp once and he obliged. I will always be grateful for that.

Legendary Coach Gene Keady

Keady had the Big Dog Glenn Robinson and Cuonzo Martin in the early 90s. Those were probably some of the better teams I had seen. Robinson was an absolute animal, averaging over 30 points per game in 1993-94 and eventually became the first pick in the NBA Draft. Robinson was on the short list of most dominant players I had the pleasure of officiating.

Purdue won the conference a handful of times during that 30 year period, but they were always solid. They had a few down years like any other program, but you could count on a tough night whenever Purdue was on the schedule. The Boilers were a solid program with great coaching stability. That won't change any time soon.

Wisconsin

Wisconsin Field House

Kohl Center

Memorable Players: Michael Finley, Kirk Penney, Devin Harris

Memorable Coaches: Bill Cofield, Dick Bennett, Bo Ryan

The old Wisconsin Field House was a beauty. It was built in 1930 and only held about 10,000 people. The thing that was interesting about it, I hated. On the way from the locker room to the floor, you had to walk through the VIP section...or something like that. It was a roped off area that we as officials walked through like zoo animals. Needless to say, the VIP section had a loaded bar and the patrons were well lubricated. We took abuse before the game, at halftime, AND after the game if the Badgers lost. I never heard so many comments about my poor mother.

Kohl Fieldhouse was completely different. Kohl was a gorgeous first-class facility that took over for the Armpit Field House in 1998. Capacity jumped to 17,000 and was a top-notch arena that is right up there with Penn State. Kohl was also used for hockey (big in Wisconsin), concerts, and other events. They did it right…it was a beautiful arena in which to watch college basketball.

Similar to Minneapolis, I didn't get up to Madison very much during the week. Most of my games there were on the weekends, or again, when my school was on Christmas Break. I would usually fly to Milwaukee and then make the 90 minute drive over to Madison.

Back when Dick Bennett was coach, the students nicknamed their student section "Mr. Bennett's Neighborhood", which eventually turned into the "Grateful Red" in 2002 when Bo Ryan took over. The student section spanned from floor to roof in 3 sections totaling about 2,100 students. They were known for their red and white vertically striped overalls and red tie-dye shirts (a la The Grateful Dead). They were a boisterous group to be sure, once ranked the #1 student section by *The Detroit News* in February of 2007.

The Badgers had six coaches during my time, starting with Bill Cofield and concluding with Bo Ryan. I particularly enjoyed Dick Bennett, as I had him a few times when he was in Green Bay. Dick was a solid guy and an excellent basketball coach. There was mutual respect between him and me.

I found Wisconsin to be very similar to Minnesota in terms of personnel. The Badgers always seemed to have big, bruising white guys that looked as if they were just pulled off the farm. They were the kind of guys you would attach the combine to and he would pull it through the field. Consequently, they played a very physical brand of basketball. You wouldn't get into a track meet with these guys…it was more of a "first team to 60 points wins". Michael Finley was the best player I saw come out of Madison, and it wasn't that close.

The Badgers were a lower tier team for a very long time, usually finishing in the bottom half of the league. Finley led them to the NCAA Tournament in 1993, breaking a 46 year drought. They finally broke through with a conference championship in 2002-03 with Kirk Penney leading the way. Times have been much better for the Badgers as of late, much better than the dreadful basketball from the 80s to mid-90s.

I offer my apologies to current Big 10 members, Maryland, Rutgers, and Nebraska. While these institutions are currently valuable members in the conference, they had not yet joined the party prior to my retirement. It goes without saying that I didn't do any Big 10 games at any of those three schools.

"I just got a text from Revlon…they thank you for the MAKE UP call."

-UMass fan

11

Best of the Best

I thought it might be fun to include a section on brother officials that I admired, the coaches I have the utmost respect for, as well as some of the top players that I had the pleasure of working with. At the end of this section, I'd also like to recognize the top contributor to our game from an official's standpoint.

Before I do that, I would be remiss if I didn't give my heartfelt sentiments to the supervisors that I worked for during my 44 years on the hardwood. As you can imagine, being a supervisor of officials is just as challenging as it sounds. It's a thankless job, but an extremely important one.

To John Adams, Lou Bonder, Bob Burson, Mickey Crowley, Jim Desmond, Rich Falk, Jim Lessig, John Payak, Herm Rohrig, and Bob Wortman… I thank you for your loyalty, commitment, and dedication to me and to the game of basketball. A heartfelt tip of the cap to you. While most of these individuals are residing in the Heaven Hall of Fame, I'm sure they still have a whistle around their necks in case the Apostles want to take on the Popes in a pickup game.

The Officials

Back to Earth and to the hardwood. As I mentioned earlier, it wasn't too often that you worked with the same guys over and over again. Needless to say, I am asked often about players and coaches, but rarely do I get many questions about fellow officials. Here are some thoughts on these guys that you probably have heard of, but don't know too much about. (By the way, this is done alphabetically, as we officials like to remain impartial!)

Dick Bestor- Dick was an all-around great guy. He was very steady and trustworthy. I worked with him countless times over my career, and I trusted him explicitly. He always held his own.

Darwin Brown- Darwin helped me get my start in the Mid-American Conference. He was very well respected by both coaches and officials alike. Darwin had excellent communication skills and had a very positive approach to the game.

Jim Burr- In my opinion, Jim is one of the best officials in the history of college basketball, and that's not an exaggeration. Jim has a knack of controlling the game from start to finish. Burr was a highly sought-after official, joining the Big Ten after spending several years as the Lead Official in the Big East.

JD Collins- I always thought JD was solid on the floor and definitely someone I trusted. A knee injury prevented him from extending his officiating career, but he eventually held the National Coordinator of Officials position in 2018.

Ed Corbett- Similar to Burr, Corbett was another official that made the jump from the Big East to the Big Ten. He had an excellent feel for the game and was very steady. I always enjoyed working with Ed.

Jim Delvecchio- I have known Jim for nearly all my life. Short of the Browns charity game, Jim is probably the most responsible for me pursuing this career. He was my former baseball coach and a Division 1 basketball official. Delvecchio assisted me at the Bova Officials Camp for over 20 years.

Bob Donato- Even if you tried really hard, it was hard to not like Bob Donato. I worked with him in several Atlantic 10 games as well as a few games in the Big Dance. Bob was a man I trusted on the floor implicitly.

Charlie Fouty- Charlie was truly the Dean of Big 10 officials. If you recall, Charlie was the gentleman that gave me some 'advice' prior to my first Big 10 game. I was fortunate to work on his crew several times early in my career. Charlie was The General on the floor. If you were on the floor with him, no one messed with you, for fear of getting Charlie's wrath.

Art McDonnell- Art was a beauty…always referred to everyone as "Coach". I always enjoyed his positivity toward the game, his work ethic, and commitment to his craft. I worked with Art during one of the Atlantic 10 Championship games.

Glenn Mayborg- Former camper, Glenn can be trusted on the floor. I'm very proud of his accomplishments.

Gary Muncy-Gary was on my first crew with Charlie Fouty during that first Indiana/Purdue game. Gary was very well respected and eventually officiated the Michigan State/Indiana State final in 1979.

Pete Pavia- Pete was one of my dearest officiating friends. Pete was an icon in the Big East. I also had the pleasure of working with him in the Atlantic 10.

Phil Robinson- Robinson was my crew chief for a number of years. Phil was a very articulate official and just a great human being. I've remained friends with Phil over the years.

Sid Rodeheffer- Sid and I always complemented each other on the floor. He was a good official that I felt never received his just due for his work.

Tom Rucker- I was fortunate to be paired with Tom and George Solomon multiple times in the Big 10. Tom was as solid as it gets. Coaches always accepted Tom's very professional manner in describing his position.

Mike Sanzere- One of the "good guys" in our profession. Mike always had a calm demeanor on the floor and the respect from the coaches. I always enjoyed him as a partner.

George Solomon- As mentioned above, I was paired with George on numerous occasions. Solomon was small in stature, but a no-nonsense referee. George had guts—never afraid to make the difficult call at home or on the road. One of my favorites to be sure.

Steve Welmer- Affectionately known as "The Big Man". Steve was very easy to get along with. I worked a ton of games with Steve. Coaches liked Steve's positive demeanor.

For my former colleagues that did NOT make this list, one of two things must have happened. One, either you were good and I simply must have forgotten about you. If that's the case, I apologize because I have worked with some great ones over the years! Or two, I DO remember you, and you couldn't referee worth a damn! I will let you decide…

The Coaches

Without question, coaches play a large part in the college game. The college game is completely different than the professional level, as these guys put in a tremendous amount of work. We only see how they perform on the basketball floor, all the behind the scenes work in recruiting, fundraising, and making sure their players make grades goes unnoticed. And let's be honest…these guys are also father figures to the teenagers that are playing for them. That's a far cry from the guys in the pro ranks who sometimes treat coaches as a necessary evil.

As officials, we realize that we are sometimes the target of frustration whether deserved or not. These coaches put in so much time and energy to their profession, and when things go sideways, it's easy to yell at the guys in the striped shirts. I tried to take that into consideration when doing ball games, and generally let things slide a bit if the disagreement in question was done in a professional manner.

With that in mind, below are some thoughts on coaches I was fortunate enough to work some games with. In my opinion, these gentlemen are among the best of the best and were guys that I had great respect for.

Tommy Amaker- Coach K did an excellent job in preparing Coach Amaker to take over a program. He was all class during his time at Michigan and Harvard. Tommy was a true gentleman and a respected teacher of young men.

Paul Biancardi- In my book, Paul was the consummate professional. One of the finest coaches in America. He was well respected for his ability to communicate with officials. ESPN thinks that highly of him too, as he is the National Recruiting Director and a basketball analyst for the Worldwide Leader..

Gayle Catlett- Gayle Catlett was a rock star in Morgantown. He paid me one of the highest compliments, "When we are on the road, I want you on the floor. I trust you, and you are fair." It doesn't get much better that that. The respect was mutual.

John Chaney- Coach Chaney was fun to work for…just as long as Calipari wasn't hanging out in the same zip code. I always respected his intensity and his work in putting Temple basketball on the map.

Mike Davis- It probably would have been easier to replace John Lennon of The Beatles, than it would be to follow Bobby Knight at Indiana. I think he did a tremendous job given the circumstances. If you had his trust, you were golden.

Dan Dakich- I always had fun with Dan, even in the heat of battle. Dan played for, and coached with, Bobby Knight before his tenure as head coach at Bowling Green. Dan is currently an ESPN color commentator.

Keith Dambrot- I had Coach Dambrot a number of times while he was on the bench for the Akron Zips. We had mutual respect for each other, making him one of my favorite coaches in the Mid-American Conference. Keith was a great teacher for the kids.

Ray Dieringer- While he didn't have the notoriety of some of the others, he was among the best in the business. Granted, I am a little biased because he helped give me my start at Cleveland State, but hey, it's my list...I can pick who I want! I will always be indebted to Coach Dieringer.

Don Donoher- Don wasn't the most heralded coaches, but in my opinion, one of the greatest coaches in the state of Ohio, leading the Dayton Flyers for 25 years. We talked basketball on a number of occasions during several golf outings. I am a big fan of his.

Steve Fisher- Steve Fisher has always been one of my favorite coaches. He was as classy an individual as any I have been around. Coach was very much in control of his teams, including during the insanity around the Fab Five days. I had many games with Coach Fisher, and I never had concern that he would treat me any less than a pure professional. In fact, at one game, he saw that I brought my son and his friend, and that their seats were three rows away from heaven. Coach intervened and had them re-seated near press row. Very classy gesture. I joked with him right before tip that he had a few calls coming his way! Utmost respect for Coach Fisher.

Jud Heathcote- Jud was an icon at Michigan State. He recruited Magic Johnson and took the Spartans to the 1979 Title game against Larry Bird, the game that was often credited as the reason why March Madness exploded in popularity. I liked Jud; he never did agree with ANY calls, but I did appreciate his intensity.

Tom Izzo- I met Coach Izzo while he was a young assistant under Heathcote. You may remember that I almost appointed him head coach during a Heathcote tirade... Tom was the perfect choice to succeed Coach Heathcote and has had great success in the program. From the first time I met him, he has remained driven and intense. I was lucky enough to have him at my camp in 1990.

Gene Keady- Coach Keady was tough, but fair. He could also be a humorist if you caught him in the right mood, or if he was up by 30. If he didn't respect you as an official, you were in for a LONG couple hours. Coach Keady also spoke at my camp in the 90s. I will always appreciate that.

Bobby Knight- You may have heard of this guy... He could get just a wee bit excitable to say the least. Coach Knight was as tough as nails and had Indiana near the top consistently during his regime. There are many mixed opinions about Coach Knight, but I would have my grandson play for him in a heartbeat.

Rollie Massimino- I first met Coach Massimino during the 1985 Hall of Fame Game. That game was just months after his incredible championship win against Georgetown, and he was as humble as could be. Very likeable Italian guy...just like yours truly!

Thad Matta- Coach Matta was a first-class guy...very respectful and professional. If Thad Matta approached you and questioned one of your calls, he was usually right—we blew it. Coach was easy to work with.

Lute Olson- Lute was one suave and debonair cat. He could appear on the cover of Gentleman's Quarterly just as easy as he could on Sports Illustrated. Hawkeye Nation loved Coach Olson, and so did fellow officials as he was easy to work with. Coach eventually left Iowa City and headed to Tucson to take over the Arizona Wildcats.

Bruce Pearl- Aside from the fiasco with Illinois/Iowa, I always thought Bruce was a good guy. I met him when he was an assistant at Iowa. Coach allowed you to do your job and work the game, and he was a great communicator to those of us in black and white.

Tubby Smith- Coach Smith was a class individual at Minnesota, and later Kentucky. Coach was a friend of the officials and allowed us to do our jobs. I remember that his teams were always well prepared.

Gary Waters- Gary was an excellent coach and leader of young men. We had our camps together at Eastern Michigan and Kent State.

Gary Williams- Gary Williams was easily one of the most intense coaches I worked with. Despite our incident at Michigan State, Coach easily makes my list. I always enjoyed how he could get the home crowd ready to blow the roof off the arena. Good guy.

The Broadcasters

Les Levine- One of the best in the Cleveland area. Les and I go WAY back as we competed against each other in high school and also in the local Triple A baseball league. Les was the voice of the Cleveland State Basketball for a number of years—including 1986 when the Vikings made their improbable tournament run, knocking off Bob Knight's Hoosiers. Since then, Les has hosted the "More Sports and Les Levine" television show on the local cable network for over 20 years.

Michael Reghi- Michael is truly one of the golden voices of college basketball and football. Reghi also served the Cleveland Cavaliers and Baltimore Orioles in play-by-play roles. We found commonality in our backgrounds, as we both had fathers that were detectives—mine in Cleveland, his in Detroit. Both were tremendous role models for us, with strong Italian values. Behind the microphone, "Reg" was always fair to the men in stripes, giving us the benefit of the doubt. To this day, Michael remains one of my very best friends.

The Players

During my 30 years in The Big 10 Conference, I had the good fortune to see many superstars perform. In my opinion, The Big 10 is as solid as any conference in America. It wasn't the up-and-down style of the Pac 12, or the finesse play of the ACC, but more of a physical, grind-it-out brand of the game. Everyone knew that a game in Big 10 country meant that you had to bring your hard hat and be ready for battle.

The conference produced a tremendous amount of talent. Some of the marquee players at the time went on to do great things in the NBA, while others will go down in history as tremendous COLLEGE players. And there's nothing wrong with that.

While it's difficult to rank players against each other, especially when considering different styles and different eras, I put together my "All-Bova" teams from my time on the court. Some selections may surprise you, as well as some omissions, but I'm a referee and I call it like I see it.

For the sake of this discussion, I will include two or three guards, and two or three front court guys for each team. Obviously, the classic 'center' position has diminished in its role since the mid-70s, but those guys shouldn't be punished for the lessened impact on today's game.

All-Bova First Team

Glenn Robinson, Purdue- "The Big Dog" was as dominant as anyone I can remember. Literally unstoppable. Averaging 30 and 10 as a Sophomore, Robinson was the Consensus National Player of the Year, before going #1 in the NBA Draft to Milwaukee. He stood out to me more than anyone in my career.

Calbert Cheaney, Indiana- The 4-year starter also was a Consensus Player of the Year in 1993. Cal averaged 20 per game for all of his seasons in Bloomington. He was a special player…one of the finest Hoosiers ever.

Clark Kellogg, Ohio State- Speaking of special, "Special K" was one of the finest high school players to come out of Ohio before a stellar career in Columbus. A steady scorer and rebounder, Kellogg was eventually the 8th pick in the NBA Draft by Indiana.

Isiah Thomas, Indiana- The All-American led the Hoosiers the National Title in 1981. Thomas was a gifted scorer and ball handler and the undisputed leader on the floor. He played only 2 seasons in Bloomington before being selected #2 in the 1981 NBA Draft.

Magic Johnson, Michigan State- What can you say about this guy? Magic truly changed basketball in being a 6 foot 7 point guard. The All-American was the best distributor of the ball I had ever seen. He had charisma, style, and unbelievable skill. Johnson led Coach Heathcote to the National Title over Larry Bird in 1979.

So, what do you think of this group? Good luck in the back court taking on these two Hall of Famers. Want a piece of "Big Dog" or "Special K"? Or take your chances against one of Bobby Knight's best ever? Put these five on the floor, and I will take on anyone.

All-Bova Second Team

Joe Barry Carroll, Purdue- Another 7 footer, who averaged 22 points and 10 boards his last two years in West Lafayette. JB was a consensus All-American before going #1 in the 1980 NBA Draft.

Michael Finley, Wisconsin- Michael Finley averaged over 20 per night for his last three seasons at Wisconsin. A good defender and slasher, Finley was a tough match up on most nights.

Jimmy Jackson, Ohio State- At 6 foot 6 inches, Jackson was as smooth as silk in the scarlet and gray. Jackson was the conference's Player of the Year twice (and UPI National Player of the Year) before leaving for the NBA after his Junior season.

Michael Redd, Ohio State- Another excellent Buckeye guard, Redd scored between 17 and 22 points in all three seasons in Columbus. The left hander had a smooth stroke…

Scott Skiles, Michigan State- I loved how tough and gritty Scott Skiles was. As a 6 foot 1 guard, Skiles averaged 27 points per game in 1985-86 en route to being named Big 10 Player of the Year.

Who wants to take on these guys? Shooters, slashers, scorers, and the #1 Pick Big Man patrolling the paint. It's an interesting mix of eras bringing JBC in from the late 70s, but his game could translate to any decade.

All-Bova Third Team

Brad Sellers, Ohio State- The 7 footer averaged 20 points and 12 rebounds in his final year at Ohio State before being a Top 10 draft choice.

Kevin McHale, Minnesota- At 6 foot 10, McHale perfected the "up and under" move and was the greatest player to come out of the Gopher program.

Glen Rice, Michigan- Rice was one of the best shooters I have ever seen. He averaged over 25 points per game in his final season at Michigan, earning conference Player of the Year honors in 1989.

Mateen Cleaves, Michigan State- Mateen Cleaves didn't do anything particularly spectacularly, but he was a tremendous leader. Cleaves was Big 10 Player of the Year TWICE while being a 40% field goal shooter. That speaks volumes.

Rumeal Robinson, Michigan- Rumeal Robinson was on the NCAA Tournament First Team when leading Michigan to the National Title in 1989. He was gritty and tough.

Not sure how a Wolverine and Spartan are going to share a ball in the backcourt, but they will figure it out. I have twin towers down low, a tremendous spot up shooter, and two guys that can act as generals on the floor while handling the rock. I will take it.

There are several guys that you could argue deserve to be on this list. Guys like Steve Alford, Steve Smith, the Fab Five, Kendal Gill, Greg Oden, Greg Stokes…I could go on and on. Suffice it to say, I have had the opportunity to officiate more than my fair share of outstanding players.

Major Contributor

People that have been in the business for a long time remember the 'old style' whistles that had the cork pea in the middle of it. If you had the pleasure to put one of those dinosaurs next to your lips, you know what I am talking about when I say that it was unappealing, unreliable, and unpredictable. My good friend and partner on the hardcourt, Ron Foxcroft, changed all that.

Ron was a well-traveled referee, having done games in the Olympics, Pan American Games, and was the first Canadian to work in Division 1 NCAA hoops. On two separate occasions, his pea whistle failed him in critical international situations, which led to rioting and brawls. He was even thrust in the middle of a situation in Brazil that could have resulted in bodily harm. Even though he tried to make the correct call, his whistle failure prevented it. He vowed to never let that happen again.

After years of research, trial and error, and near financial ruin, Ron developed the "pea-less" whistle that produced a remarkable sound, proper decibel, and worked with 100% consistency. Modeled after a church pipe organ, the 3-chamber unit did not rely on the position of a cork ball, and it would not fail with saliva buildup. It was a work of art.

The Fox 40 whistle quickly became the industry standard. Today, it's used in every major professional sport, by police, the coast guard, crisis centers, you name it. In total, Foxcroft's brilliance led to tens of millions of Fox 40 whistles being sold in over 140 countries.

As a basketball official, you don't have much equipment to count on in order to perform your duties. Short of proper referee attire and a good pair of shoes, your whistle is your best friend. Foxcroft helped make sure that every referee in every situation had a tool they could count on to perform their job properly.

Personally, Ron and I have remained friends long after our time on the floor. He was kind enough to make the trip down from Ontario to attend my Hall of Fame ceremony, something I will forever be grateful for. In a similar way, referees all over the world should be grateful for Ron's contribution to the game and to society as a whole.

"People have gotten pregnant with less contact than that!"

-Iowa Fan

12

<u>Times are A-changing</u>

It's interesting—I watch the game now and see how much different things are than they were a few decades ago. The style of play is different, the demeanor of the officials is different, and the national interest in the game has increased. I'll explain what I mean here shortly, but I'm not even sure that is possible.

The college game, and really the pro game too, has evolved tremendously. Gone are the days of the traditional 'back to the basket' centers. Guys like Patrick Ewing and Hakeem Olajuwon that were so dominant don't exist anymore. Instead, 7-footers are judged on how well they can run the floor, handle the ball and shoot from the outside. Look at Durant. Look at Nowitzki. Back in the 80s, guys like that would be parked in the paint and taught post moves. Maybe Magic Johnson started the revolution of guys not being pigeon holed to positions because of size, but now positions are almost interchangeable. Even in the NBA, they used to vote for two guards, two forwards, and a center for the All Star Teams. Now it's three frontcourt guys and two guards. The stereotypical center is like Bigfoot. You hear he's out there, but you can't see him anywhere.

When the NCAA instituted the shot clock for the 1985 season, and the 3-point shot the year after, the little guy was officially welcomed back to the game. Prior to the shot clock, pace of play could be painful. Dean Smith's "Four Corners" could put you to sleep. Sure, it got the job done in the right situation, but it wasn't fun to watch. Similarly, teams could limit the amount of possessions in a game, put an aircraft carrier in the Center position, and let him lumber down the floor and drop anchor in the key. The introduction of the shot clock forced faster play and forced players to be in better shape as they had to get up and down the floor so many more times. Increased possessions led to more offseason conditioning and training, which led to these giants running the floor like gazelles.

In a similar way, the 3-point line put a premium on guys who could shoot the ball from the outside. I wasn't a math major, but if you could get three points on a possession as opposed to two, why wouldn't you? That logic has caused the game to be much more spread out, and consequently a bit easier on the officials. Prior to the trifecta, the game was very compact with a lot of bodies in a smaller area. When you think about it, officials have become more concerned on whether someone's toe was on the line instead of making the '3 seconds in the paint' call. How often does that get called anymore? Not too often....why? Rarely is anyone parked there anymore!

Of course, this has an impact on the officials too. Referees calling the game need to be in better shape than ever before. It was taxing enough to run the floor with the college kids when games were 53-50, but now that scores are typically in the 70s and 80s, it's a lot more wear and tear on the body.

To that point, I recall officials being much more demonstrative when calling infractions. I was as guilty as anyone. We made the call with conviction, and 'sold' the call with emphasis. Now it seems guys make the call in a very non-chalant manner, almost as if going through the motions. Not sure why. Maybe it's a result of the further scrutiny that officials are under?

Maybe guys want to 'blend' in more and not be a focal point? I get it...officials should never be part of the story, but making calls with conviction helps eliminate any doubt from either team that the correct call was made.

While the game has changed significantly in style of play, if I ruled the NCAA basketball universe, there would be some changes that I would make to the game. I'm pretty sure nobody will be giving me the keys to the kingdom, but here are a couple things that make sense to me....

The alternating possession rule stinks. I would go back to the days of an ACTUAL jump ball if there was a tie up. The rule went into effect in 1981 and has had supporters and detractors. People that support the alternating possession say that small players will rarely—if ever—win an actual jump ball and not get rewarded for their effort. If 5 foot 3 Muggsy Bogues tied somebody up, would he win too many jump balls? Probably not. Or-if a team could put anyone they wanted in the circle to jump, a skyscraper or jumping jack would win the tip every time. On the other side of the fence, if a team makes a tremendous play to tie someone up during crunch time when they NEED to get the ball back in the closing seconds, they are at the mercy of the pointing arrow on the scorer's desk. I don't like that. Get rewarded for your efforts and hustle and give your team the opportunity for a shot at possession. Jump ball to start the game, other team gets possession at the start of the 2nd half, and actual jump balls in between. Makes sense to me.

The other thing I would change is personal fouls when a game goes to overtime. In the NCAA, it's five fouls in 40 minutes before disqualification. In the NBA, it's six fouls in 48, before you get sent to the pine. Both organizations seem to agree that one foul every eight minutes is the correct allotment. So, if a game goes to overtime…or two overtimes, the amount of fouls allowed per player doesn't change. Why not? A team gets an additional time out when going to the extra session, so why shouldn't players that survived the first 40 minutes be allowed to have an additional foul? Survival is the key word…if you reached five fouls in regulation time, in my world, you are done for the day. Games that go to overtime were obviously tight toward the end, which may have included ADDITIONAL fouling to even get to the overtime period. Now you want kids to play an extra five or ten minutes (or more) without the benefit of an added foul to give? That makes no sense to me. Coaches should be able to use their normal arsenal of players (within reason) to decide games. They shouldn't have to suit up the water boy and athletic trainer in a 4-overtime game because everyone has five fouls. A 4-overtime game equates to an additional HALF of basketball…and you want kids to still only have five fouls in their tool belt? That makes no sense either.

The game has been tweaked so many times since Dr. Naismith nailed that peach basket to the wall. While I don't see any major or significant changes coming, I'm pretty sure things will continue to get fine-tuned. After all, changes and improvements are made for the benefit of that athlete as well as for the enjoyment of the fan, while keeping the integrity of the game intact. College basketball is a multi-gazillion dollar business, and the NCAA definitely needs the support of television right, advertising sponsorships, and most importantly, FANS of the game to continue doing what it's doing at the highest level.

When I first started in the 70s, the game was popular, but not to the extent that it is now. The regular season gets overshadowed a bit by the shadow of the NFL, but come March, there's nothing like NCAA hoops. I've said a few times that the Magic vs Bird championship game in 1979 really exploded the popularity of the tournament, and I really believe that to be true.

Fans are still loyal to the school that they went to or the in-state university when following hoops. It's tough to latch onto actual players anymore, as the 1-and-done rule has robbed college hoops of the icons that were so frequent in years past. When you think of great performances in the tournament...like Carmelo at Syracuse or Anthony Davis at Kentucky, it's rare that they stick around for more than that explosive first year. Both were MVPs of the tournament as freshmen, but the allure of the NBA was too great for them to continue playing for their schools. How would college hoops history be different if players actually played for 3-4 years instead of bolting to the pros? It has gotten to the point that we root for the laundry of the school running up and down the floor, because the actual bodies in those uniforms change so frequently.

In either case, the drama of the games is tremendous for even the casual sports fan. Come tournament time, office pools all over America sprout up to have a piece of the action. Companies are offering millions of dollars in exchange for the submission of a "perfect bracket". What are the two busiest weekends in Las Vegas? Super Bowl weekend and the opening round of March Madness always pack those mega-hotels to the rafters. Certainly, gambling has something to do with that, but baseball offers 15 games every day; there's no popularity explosion there? Now that sports gambling has been legalized in states that choose to offer it, I believe the popularity of college basketball and the tournament specifically will continue to rise.

Gambling has always been a touchy subject in relation to sports. The guys in the desert have an incredible ability to come up with the 'number' that—more often than not—hovers around the final score. As a former official, it absolutely amazes me that some folks think we have an eye on the point spread when working a game. That's ludicrous. This is our job, our livelihood. To think that officials care about the final score of a ball game is almost insulting. We are more concerned about making the correct calls, doing our job to the best of our abilities, and getting out of town to prepare for the next game. With the increased availability of sports wagering, there is no doubt in my mind that there will be increased scrutiny on those wearing stripes.

I can honestly say that I have never been approached once in regard to the point spread. Did I make calls at the end of a game that COULD have swayed a point spread winner one way or another? No idea…but I'm sure I did? It would be nearly impossible not to. I had too much going on in controlling a game than to have any regard to what a final score might be. I go to sleep every night with a very clear conscience.

As for the officiating profession today, we are losing more and more people. We need good talent to continue to come through the system and replace the men and women that have done it for years.

Why the shortage? It's pretty simple in my view. The baby boomers are retiring, and the new wave of officials take way too much abuse from coaches and wacko parents. The working environment (especially at the youth level) has become much more difficult. The pounding on referees now just isn't something that a lot of folks want to deal with.

To truly advance up the ladder, full time jobs have become much more time demanding and prevent some of the better officials of working two occupations at the same time. If you are trying to raise a family, the time commitment is tremendous. Not everyone is as blessed as I was to have Donna by my side.

Consequently, many folks are content working the local Division 3 circuit. Those games come with less pressure, less abuse, and less travel. My best advice for new officials is to set realistic goals, be patient, and lean on the support of your family.

Lastly, the politics involved in getting games assigned has turned people off. You almost need a 'godfather' in the business to take you under his wing and help you advance to where you want to go. Many leagues have Referee Camps that you MUST attend to even be considered…and at that, you are lucky to even be invited for a chance to throw your hat in the ring. It's a cut-throat business for sure.

All told, the state of college basketball is as good right now as it has ever been. There's no reason to think that there is anything to slow down this locomotive for years to come.

"It's about time you called a hold...they have been doing that ALL GAME LONG!"

-Michigan State Fan (with 19.18 minutes left in FIRST half)

13

Blessed and Proud

Needless to say, I have been incredibly blessed and fortunate to have the career and experiences that I have had. You just never know where life is going to take you! To think that all this started because I decided to go to a Cleveland Browns vs Faculty charity basketball game is really mind boggling when you stop and think about it.

During my career, I've had the good fortune to meet a tremendous amount of people, see much of the country, and witness some of the finest basketball players in the world on an up close and personal basis. I'm not naïve enough to think that there aren't millions of other guys in the country that would have jumped at the chance to experience all that I have.

As they say, Father Time is undefeated, and all things must eventually come to an end. It's a wonder how 44 years in the NCAA can go so quickly and in the blink of an eye. With the dozens of sports channels available carrying classic games from the past, I occasionally still see myself on TV and remember fondly what it was like to be in environments like that.

Make no mistake, while I am very proud of my longevity on the hardwood, I am also very proud of a number of different things that don't involve my whistle. On the educational side, I was fortunate enough to earn "Educator of the Year" honors for

my work at Buckeye High School. That recognition is something I
was ecstatic to earn, as I poured my heart and soul into the kids at
that school. I was also named to the Medina County Sports Hall of
Fame and the Greater Cleveland Sports Hall of Fame for my
athletic achievements, community service and successful career as
a college official.

Greater Cleveland Hall of Fame Ceremony

     Both are honors that I treasure. To be named to a Hall with
such Cleveland legends as Bob Feller, Jim Brown, and the like…it
was truly special.

     Furthermore, off the hardwood, the Bova Baseball Camp
remains a pride and joy. Harkening back to my days on the
diamond, I started the Bova Baseball Camp for youths in 1973 and
have had the camp EVERY YEAR since then. 2018 marked the
45th consecutive year that youths from 7 to 14 years of age will

better themselves on the field with instruction from me and my staff. That camp has given me tremendous joy for nearly five decades.

Extremely Proud of our Baseball Staff!

Currently, along with Mike and Bob D'Andrea, I am one of the owners and investors of T3 (Test, Teach, Train) Performance in Avon, Ohio. The 56,000 square foot complex offers state-of-the-art equipment and facilities, working in conjunction with University Hospitals. Physical therapy and rehabilitation services are offered there too. It's a fabulous facility. Helping athletes train SMARTER, and not necessarily HARDER, gives our team great satisfaction.

Groundbreaking at the T3 Facility

Saving the best for last, the thing I am most proud of is my family. My mother and father, Helen and Phil, were true blue collar parents. They set the example and laid the foundation for the values I treasure today. Hard work. Commitment. Loyalty. I have often said that if I could be half the man my father was, it would be a great accomplishment. I hope I have made you proud, Mom and Dad.

I could not complete this book without sharing my thoughts about my brother Frank, also a former Cleveland detective. Frank was my best friend and confidant for many games. He was my biggest fan, but also my biggest critic. Because of his wisdom and understanding of people, he helped me to keep my priorities in perspective. I will always be grateful for his support and guidance

My daughters, Michelle and Jennifer, and son Michael each have three children. In total, nine grandchildren—five boys and four girls. Donna and I refer to them as the Divine Nine. Watching them grow up and compete in sports brings me great joy. More often than not, I find myself biting my tongue while watching them play. Why is that, you ask?

The officiating stinks!

Donna has been my rock for over 51 years and has been nothing but loving and supportive. We have shared so many ups and downs, highs and lows that I simply could not have had the career I have had without her. I started this section by saying how blessed I was to have had the experiences I have had, but I am TEN TIMES more blessed to have the family I do. I will enjoy my children and grandchildren for as long as the Good Lord allows me.

Whatever your dream is, chase it! **EMBRACE YOUR PASSION**!!! Make the most of it. Keep your eyes open for opportunity. You just never know when you will be presented with something that might change your life forever. Do your best and take pride in what you do. Love your family and those around you, and good things will happen. The Lord works in mysterious ways.

When the opportunity does present itself, follow the advice of my friend and mentor, Charlie Fouty…and I will tone it down…

Don't SCREW it up!

Donna and I

Michelle and Dave   **Jennifer and Jeff**   **Mike and Kelly**

The Divine 9!

A Closer Look at the Bov...

Full Name: Phillip Michael Bova

Family: Wife Donna, Three Children, Nine Grandchildren

Car: White Chevy Suburban

Hobbies: Golf, Bowling, Boating and Watching my
    Grandchildren compete

Favorite TV Show: - "The Honeymooners" with Jackie Gleason

Favorite Movie: - "The Godfather"

Favorite Actor/Actress: Jimmy Cagney, Robert De Niro, and
    Lucille Ball

Favorite Athlete: Arnold Palmer

Favorite Song: - "That's Amore" by Dean Martin

Favorite Number: 3

Best Compliment I Received: - "You are a loyal and committed
    person"

Best Advice I Ever Received: - "To complete my master's
    degree"

Worst Advice I Ever Received: - "I was too young to get married
    to my high school love." 52 years and counting in 2019

My Perfect Day: Spending time at the lake with my family

Favorite Way to Give Back to Kids: - (see next page!)

For 44 years, I played Santa for the Buckeye Schools kids. This
picture of me made the cover of Referee Magazine

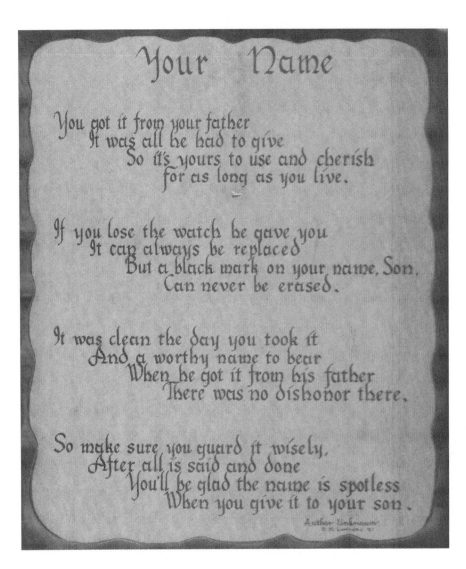

Your Name

You got it from your father
It was all he had to give
So it's yours to use and cherish
for as long as you live.

If you lose the watch he gave you
It can always be replaced
But a black mark on your name, Son,
Can never be erased.

It was clean the day you took it
And a worthy name to bear
When he got it from his father
There was no dishonor there.

So make sure you guard it wisely,
After all is said and done
You'll be glad the name is spotless
When you give it to your son.

Author Unknown

Very Important to me. Words to live by

ABOUT THE AUTHOR

Nino Frostino is a lifelong Clevelander, Miami of Ohio graduate, and avid sports fan. Nino grew up down the street from the Bovas and their families have been life-long friends. Fascinated by Phil's memories on the hardcourt, Nino vigorously pursued Phil to put these stories on paper. Finally in 2018, the two committed to the project. This is Nino's second sports book, as **Right on the Numbers** was released in 2003. He is very proud of **Throwing Back the Chair**, and it is his distinct honor to chronicle what he has heard and witnessed his entire life.

Made in the USA
Middletown, DE
15 February 2022

61226019R00120